The Faith Principle

4 Secrets to Making Your Faith Work For You Again

By Don Mingo

Copyright © Donald James Mingo 2020

ISBN 978-1-7323525-3-7

10 9 8 7 6 5 4 3 2 1

Published in 2020
by
Mingo Coaching Group LLC
Grandbury, Texas USA

Cover Design by Daniel Mingo

donmingobooks@gmail.com

Why?

Why another book about faith? What can an author possibly add to that which others have written about so profusely over the last 1900 years? The answer: this is a book about my discoveries of faith; how faith became real to me. A very private journey is shared within these pages.

There's a simple principle of faith in the Bible. A principle that turns faith into real experience beyond talking points and sermons. Where faith shakes off the dust of doubt to live and breathe. A faith that connects us to God in tangible ways.

This faith does not appear the experience of many – if not most – who attend church, sit in small groups, or maybe participate in Bible studies. Or, among the wandering tribes of people who left the church abandoning faith entirely.

Faith-strugglers who desire a better experience look to spiritual communities for adhesion of faith to God. Often, they experience separation from God.

And, of course, there are the many church attenders who seem to own no functional faith outside, "This is what I believe."

This book describes a faith that adequately explains why we believe what we believe. A faith that works. Is active. Is real. A faith that matters in my life and yours. That kind of faith.

In endless interactions with people about faith, one constant stands out regardless of denominational affiliation or faith community. Whether Pentecostal, Baptist, Catholic, Free Church, orthodox, traditional or mega-church, people struggle with faith.

Two faith spheres appear to exist for many of us.

A first level resembles a pronouncement. A defining of that which one claims to believe. "I believe in…" is foundational to what a person understands about what they try to believe.

It is the second plane that *The Faith Principle* seeks to reveal. A faith existing adorned in the Bible like gold waiting to be unearthed by a curious prospector. I like to refer to this kind of faith as evidential faith. Evidential faith is faith that adds, "I believe because…"

The question I love to ask people as I travel and speak is, "How is your faith real to you?" As many stutter, their answer usually comes out something like, "This is what I believe." The "what" they believe replaces the "how it's' real" and "why" they believe it.

It's wonderful to believe in what you believe, but why do you believe what you believe?

My next question equally confounds: "How does your faith help you believe in God?" The sputtering as people search for an answer is astounding.

A quick answer often comes, "Because the Bible says so, or that's what our church teaches, or that's what I've always believed."

Ok, good. Adequate? No.

The Faith Principle tries to answer both the "what" and "why" of faith. Many talk about what they believe. Far fewer can express why they actually believe it. From experience, this is true with regular church attenders, church leaders, and Christian organizations.

In my journey these past sixty-two years, I've observed countless numbers of people – including myself – who expressed frustration with a faith they sincerely try to believe, but stand looking at a disappointing hollow chasm of experience. Those shoes are not comfortable.

It's not that people don't believe in faith, but rather that their faith doesn't carry much practical benefit for them.

The Faith Principle talks about faith's frustrations, when faith doesn't seem to work. When attending church services feels senseless. When prayer seems like a wasteful exercise of talking to yourself. When we become spiritually disconnected from God while trying to believe in God.

The Faith Principle discusses a practical faith. Faith that can and does work when understanding and following a very simple principle laid down in the Bible.

The Faith Principle uncovers a truth among truths regarding faith. Faith is not faith simply because one believes or possesses it. Faith is faith because of the object it looks upon to trust.

The Faith Principle marks a reawakening of my own faith. After countless frustrations – regardless of personal efforts – my faith began to break free from its long-worn chrysalis on a day I like to call "That Day."

That Day

God compensates sincere genuine faith in Him.

— The Faith Principle

This is a story of faith. My faith. That's not to say I've got it all figured out. Or, that my faith exhibits a virtue beyond anyone else's. Far from it.

This is my account of how after many years my faith began to connect to belief. In doing so, faith finally began to make sense to me.

This is also about a faith written in the pages of the Bible. I'm not the first to discover *The Faith Principle*.

This story – my story – is simply an uncovering of an old truth – a principle – that works for me as it worked for others in the past. A truth I know can work for you too.

It's a story of talking about something for decades, then finally beginning to understand of that which I spoke. It happened on a day I like to call "That Day."

That Day

There was no hint when standing before almost 100 missionaries that day in Central America that our lives would take an unimaginable turn back to the thing I'd fled. That Day whispered a hint of change. An inexplicable detour from our dream life in Northern Minnesota.

Returning from over twenty years of missionary service among the Zulus in South Africa, we – Kathy and me – sought for a settling down. A place to take a deep breath. Get away from the many wonderful and horrible things we experienced. To live our last chapters of life winding down from it all.

Burrowed in the woods of Northern Minnesota, the withdrawal and serenity offered me hope to deal with PTSD's ravages upon my person, our relationship, and my soul.

Sure, it's cold way up there near the Canadian border. But, seclusion surpassed dealing with 50 below zero-degree temperatures in the winter. There, I could disappear into the woods, or on the lakes with my camera, boat and journals.

With help from wonderful people of the church I pastored, we built a small yellow house in the woods. I loved my house and purposed to never move again. That Day changed my intents and expectations.

Tim – a missionary in Central America – asked me to speak at their annual missionary retreat in Central America. There I stood that day in Siguatepeque, Honduras before a wonderful group of weathered missionaries. People I didn't know.

Standing before the group of friendly strangers, I intended to deliver my prepared talk on endurance. Looking at the audience, my first words sputtered. A shift of intent occurred.

Abandoning my notes, and looking that day at those missionaries, a glimpse into their souls pried my guarded heart open. I thought, "They're in the same boat as me."

Taking a deep breath, I tried to bring up that buried in my mind and soul for years. Stumbling through at a bare whisper, they heard my story of a crumbling. A coming to an end of myself in South Africa. Reaching a point of emotional debilitation. The need to return to the United States. To find a way to look at people again without suspicion, fear – and worse – indifference.

There, for the first time, I tried to share my PTSD story. A story my therapist and a few close friends warned me not to tell. Reactions of others towards those with PTSD often borders on fear, suspicion and apprehension. This seems especially true in faith communities. People tend to go a bit medieval on you at the mention of PTSD, mental illness or a breakdown.

Of all the incidents, I chose to talk about Andiswa. The worst story that disfigured my soul involved a most precious little Zulu girl. Her trauma of being raped at two years of age. Contracting AIDS and dying with her little fingers clinging to my index finger with eyes wide open as she took her last breath.

I ended my first talk on that day with, *I'm just a missionary, speaking to missionaries, about missionary things. You are my heroes.* That Day changed me. I just didn't understand how much.

On the last day of that Missionary Retreat, we watched dozens of missionaries pack their vehicles and head back to their humble homes. Missionaries who shared horrendous stories of valor serving throughout Honduras trying to help orphans, street children, the homeless, and the abandoned while living on the drug highways of Central America.

Flying back to Minneapolis St. Paul Airport, we put our luggage into the truck and began a three-hour journey home. Arriving at our newly built home in the woods, I stopped at the entrance of the driveway.

I loved this house built by my congregation. We painted it the same color as my great-grandparents' cabin on a lake thirty minutes away. A cabin long ago abandoned by our family at the passing of grandpa and grandma. A cabin which existed mostly in memories.

I loved the woods. The lakes. Fishing. Photography. And, our yellow house. Standing in the driveway looking through the thick clusters of trees, that yellow house peered out from the dense forest as if to say, "What are you doing here?"

I slipped my arm around Kathy and said, "You know what sweetie?" Looking up at me, she smiled and said, "We need to let it go." I chuckled, "Yep." But, I didn't want to release my beautiful little yellow house in the woods.

A thought followed, "God, if we take this new step – giving this all up – towards another unclear direction, will it be worth it? Change again? Another transition? Another move?"

That day began to show me the value of genuine faith. Faith that brings ugly pieces of a time together weaving them into a beautiful tapestry of life. A thread giving pain a reason to exist. A purpose to pursue. A fresh breath in stale air. An inkling of excitement – long ago vanished – to the rising of a new day.

That Day redirected. As water gliding over a waterfall catching the rays of sunlight forming colorful prisms of light, That Day opened new depths of hope.

That Day… ah… that day would produce a fresh personal look into faith. I call this journey *The Faith Principle*.

The Faith Principle states:

God compensates sincere genuine faith in Him.

Ponderings

I like the word "ponder." It describes my thoughts and musings. To ponder – for me – is to wander. Wandering through my soul and mind meditating and digesting possibilities.

Pondering is a more apt description of my inner processes than "wander." Yet, pondering also limits contemplation to a single course of thoughtfulness.

Like the wanderings of Odysseus, my pondering branches out on many mental journeys.

Ponderings better fits my explorative mind. Grammar frowns on adding an "s" to the end of the word. "Ponderings is not a word!" I'm told.

Well, for me, it is. Therefore, at the end of many chapters I present several ponderings for your reflection. Ponderings that perhaps don't offer an easy path of pensive reflection.

What ponderings offers is a deep-sea diving expedition into your soul. It's up to you how deep you wish to journey.

Ponderings

→ The Faith Principle States, "God compensates sincere genuine faith in Him." Your thoughts?

→ Have you experienced any "That Days" of your own?

→ How does your "That Days" affect faith?

- 3 -

The Compensator

When sharing this principle, a friend objected, "God doesn't owe me anything. He doesn't need to compensate me for believing in him."

I replied, "In fact, God does compensate us in our attempts to move towards Him in faith," explaining that a rare word used in the Bible connected with faith implies, "*to compensate.*"

*... Anyone who wants to come to him must believe that God exists and that he **rewards (compensates)** those who sincerely seek him.*

— Hebrews 11:6 Emphasis Mine

Rewards

The word "rewards" here in Hebrews 11:6 comes from the Greek word "misthapodotēs." This word is rare in the New Testament as it's only used one time.

In most English translations the word used to express "misthapodotēs" is "rewards." It's an accurate enough word, but our modern usage of the word stunts our ability to appreciate its incredible truth.

When we think of receiving a reward, it often carries a connotation of giving of a gift in recognition of a courteous act. One receives a reward for returning a lost puppy. Finding a misplaced wallet. We receive a reward for giving information.

You often see a sign or a request on Facebook exclaiming, "Reward given for the return of…"

Countries offer rewards to anyone offering information leading to the capture of a fugitive.

That's not exactly what going on here in Hebrews 11:6.

Compensates

According to The *New American Standard Hebrew-Aramaic and Greek Dictionaries* by Robert L. Thomas, this unique Greek word defines God in relationship to our faith. God is one who pays wages.[1] God becomes a compensator or recompenser based upon our faith connection with him.

When we sincerely seek God it brings God pleasure. In return, he becomes our *misthapodotēs* – rewarder – the one who pays wages by compensating us for sincere genuine faith.

Stepping towards God in faith brings God's compensation. Little faith, little compensation. Better faith, better compensation. More faith, more compensation.

God does this because when we focus our faith upon Him, he becomes the source of that faith. Material possessions, affluency, or prestige doesn't present a conflict in worship when God is embedded in faith.

The purpose of The Book of Hebrews was to encourage persecuted people of faith not to give up on God and relapse into unbelief.[2] Paul assured them that their faith and continual seeking after God would result in God's compensation even in their suffering.

Rewards Vs. Compensation

The Faith Principle is not another book about Health and Wealth Theology. Give God a little, and he makes you a happy ageless millionaire surrounded by friends, family, and an eternally gorgeous or handsome spouse. No, this is not that kind of book. Because, that kind of faith is not the faith of the Bible contrary to popular teachings today.

More stuff. Better health. A nicer vehicle. A fat retirement. Better relationships. Happiness and significance. In this, faith appears more of a bartering with God for that which one wants. It places an individual at the center of faith rather than God. And, it fosters idolatry.

Biblical scholars argue whether the compensation-reward referred to in Hebrews 11:6 refers to only the person of God rather than what we receive from God. Yes, God alone is our reward. Our compensator. But God is also at the core of any reward because God is the Compensator of faith.[3] It appears to me that this verse refers to both: God's person and God's provisions.

These two opposites – who God is and what God gives – connect in the middle unraveling the secrets of a compensating rewarding faith.

The Faith Principle seeks this connection. The more we seek God the more God is pleased. God responds by compensating us with his **presence**, **pleasure**, **person** and **presents**.

Compensates, because the path of faith is often strewn with challenges, hardships, and suffering for the people of faith.

Compensates because like Moses who by faith chose affliction over the hedonism of his day. Faith calls us to do the same today. — Hebrews 11:25

Compensates because the destination of faith far surpasses the expressions and experiences of the moment. — Hebrews 11:39-40

Compensates because faith dissipates fear. — Matthew 8:26

Compensates because faith casts a long shadow over our doubts. — Matthew 17:20; 21:21

Compensates because faith breathes life into unbelief. — Hebrews 4:2

Compensates because faith promises an inheritance not touched by mortality and momentary troubles. — Hebrews 6:12

Compensates because faith delivers a good report on the behalf of faith-bearers. — Hebrews 11:39

By faith I am able to enter the very presence of God. As I chose to pursue God, my *misthapodotēs* – God – showers me with compensating rewards.[4] Both in this existence and the next.

No, I'm not speaking of a 10-million-dollar house, yacht or Ferrari 458. Not that kind of rewards. Rather, a compensation of the desires of the heart seated in a pursuance of God.

Delight yourself in the Lord and he will give you
the desires of your heart.

— Psalm 37:4 ESV

Faith is a dynamic exchange with God rather than a tiresome doing for God. Not a faith solely motivated by behavior, but inspired by belonging.[5] In belonging believing. In believing receiving. In receiving becoming. In becoming, owning a faith that is real.

My Compensator

Selling our beloved home in Northern, Minnesota and entering the ranks of the unemployed at 57 years of age, we sought God in our next steps. I sat houseless. Free of any entanglements. Debt free.

After moving in with our oldest son, his wonderful wife and kidos, we went to Branson, Missouri for a couple weeks of decompressing. This marked seven months after That Day in Central America.

I reconnected with Jon in Springfield, Missouri. He directs the missionary agency we served under for more than twenty years while serving as missionaries in South Africa. The intention of my visit was to reconnect with a friendly chat. Sitting down with Jon in his office, I attempted to share "That Day."

Jon spoke first. "Don," he said, "I've got an idea." He continued, "I'd like to call it Missionary to Missionaries."

The concept was simple. Weathered battled tested missionaries with training, skills, and a story of overcoming, would come alongside missionaries out in the fields and trenches of service.

We'd need to raise our own finances to fund the new endeavor. With zero income, no house and a beat-up old car, we launched out, content with God at our helm.

Our struggles prepared us for such an endeavor. I thought, "God, you can't be this good." The woods of Northern Minnesota began to lose its luster when looking at the opportunities and challenges before us.

Like a miner looking into deep shaft for gold, a rich vein of ore began to appear. It took time, pain, and hard work to uncover. As I roughed out the principle in my journal, I wrote:

In all the hardships of this life
God, you are my Compensator.

Ponderings

→ How does God compensate you for faith?

→ Or, how do you feel faith is not compensated?

→ What are your faith rewards?

→ Your faith disappointments?

– 4 –

Faith, So What?

*And it is **impossible** to please God **without Faith**.*

— Hebrews 11:6

Once a frustrated church member tried to push a conversation with our leaders towards what he deemed a more important direction for the church. The issue involved the availability of the facilities for use by what he called, "It's core members." Core members held status over regular attenders.

He exclaimed, "We pay for all of this! Why can't we use it when we want it?" "Use it," involved setting up a Saturday Swap Shop in the gymnasium for sportsmen to gather and sell their sports memorabilia for profit. The church – as a 501c3 not-for-profit organization – might find an increased interest by the IRS in such a venture.

Trying to redirect the conversation towards faith. I asked, "Fred, how does faith figure into this?" In his often-explosive manner he erupted, "Faith!? Faith!? So what!"

I replied, "Well, faith is a big deal. In fact, it's the highest and first consideration."

He huffed, "Well, not with me!"

I pressed, "Fred, will this please God?"

He answered, "I don't know."

My next answer ended the conversation, "Fred, apart from faith nothing pleases God. If you can show us the faith-factor in this activity, we can give it some thought and come up with a plan, perhaps."

It's not that we didn't care about sportsmen. Or, sportswomen for the matter. In Northern Minnesota, many women love to hunt and fish as much as men. But we already conducted many events each year for sports people. Each event was bathed in faith and prayer.

The aim above all was to please God with every event we conducted. There is only one factor that accomplishes this: faith. Not the busyness of church programs and activities. Neither devout Bible reading and prayer. Apart from faith, nothing pleases God.

The writer of Hebrews did not say it's difficult to please God without faith. He says **it's absolutely Impossible**.

Let's get a hold of this for a moment. Impossible.

I once asked a group of wonderful Zulu Christians outside of Ladysmith, South Africa, "How do you please God?" Surprisingly, their answers resembled those of the people in the church I pastored in Minnesota.

Go to church every week. Give your offering. Read your Bible. Love people. Join the church. Get baptized. Pray.

Absent of every comment was any concept of faith. Yet, according to the Bible faith is everything.

Faith is a big deal. Why? Because all the good activities we involve ourselves in doesn't gain God's favor apart from it. Faith is the only single ingredient required to achieve God's pleasure.

If our efforts fall short of faith, and if faith results in receiving reciprocal compensation from God, then faith is the vein of gold we must seek. Every experience with God hangs upon this.

Ponderings

→ How does faith help you?

→ How do you feel your faith has let you down?

→ Can you explain your faith to someone?

→ Faith – your faith – so what?

Faith's
Intangible Tangibles

Any faith that admires truth, that strives to know God,
must be brave enough to accommodate the universe.

— Carl Sagan, Contact

Space exploration fascinates me. For example, NASA's Cassini probe has discovered deep lakes on Saturn's moon – Titan – according to space reporter Erin Winick in the April 17, 2019 edition of MIT Technology Review.

As a God-seeker, I'm interested in what science is discovering. Space exploration constantly points me towards a higher being. An intelligent being. A creator. All that is out there in the vast cosmos points me beyond randomness to design.

The remarkable Hubble telescope gives us the tiniest of glimpses into a seemingly endless universe. It propels us to see, discover, and explore further space mysteries.

With the 2021 launch date of the James Webb Space Telescope, and the upcoming Artemis program to land astronauts on the moon as a steppingstone to eventual exploration of Mars, space advances points towards the amazing possibilities of what awaits us out there.

Yet, in all of our technological advances where are we today? China, Russia, and the United States militarize at alarming rates. A dozen countries possess nuclear capabilities.

Weapons from doomsday submarines capable of launching nuclear drones,[6] or developing anti-satellites (ASAT) to destroy each other's satellites overshadows our attempts to find cures for diseases.

As we seek to discover more, we appeared doomed to self-destruction. The trillions of dollars spent on wars might easily find a cure for cancer. Feed every person on the planet. Provide clean water for all the earth's inhabitants.

Seems to me that a dose of "created in the image of God" and Jesus words, "Love one another," is exactly what this world desperately needs today. Faith is such a portal to find that better hope.

Criticisms cry that that which faith-bearers claim to believe cannot possibly hold true because faith is intangible. The empirical minds and methods of the day cry foul, "You can't see faith, you can't touch faith, you can't put it under a microscope, carbon-14 data test it, and so on. Yet…

The Evidence of things not seen in Hebrews 11:1 marks this generation more than any other. The first telescope made by German-Dutch lens maker Hans Lippershey in 1608[7] gave evidence of a cosmos which ancients wondered about for centuries.

The development of the marvelous Hubble and Kepler Telescopes cracked open our door – if only slightly – to what's out there in the universe. Until the Hubble was launched, we didn't know of the existence of any planets beyond our own Solar System.[8]

The more we learn about the planets, solar systems and galaxies, the more we realize how little we understand about the rapidly expanding universe.[9] A universe expanding far faster than previously estimated leaving some scientists scratching their heads. Other mysteries exist.

A star known as the "Methuselah star" – scientifically called HD 140283 – is situated about 200 light years away. This recent Hubble Telescope discovery stumps experts as they search for answers.

It appears to many in the scientific community that this star is 16 billion years old. This challenges the Big Bang Theory which estimates the universe is only 13.8 billion years old. Studies, postulations, and theories seek agreement with this paradox.[10]

Through the lenses of telescopes and cameras we now study the existence of that which until only recently was unseen. Faith is like that.

Faith makes God visible. Just as the Hubble Telescope realized that four additional moons exist circling Pluto, the lens of faith's passionate intuition makes it possible to grasp God.

Faith is the lens by which we see the reality of what we hope to be truth: God. Yet, modernists grunt their disapproval. How can you believe in it if you can't see it?

In the 1997 film adaptation of Carl Sagan's novel *Contact,* a battle between faith and science unfolds. I thought the book and movie a very honest discussion between the minds of science and faith.

In the movie, Joss Palmer – a progressive clergy member – played by Matthew McConaughey, poses a question to atheist Radio Astronomer Eleanor Arroway played by Jodie Foster.

The conversation heats up about the possibility of the existence of God as Ellie says, "I read your book. Would you like me to quote you?"

She cites, "Ironically the thing that people are most hungry for – meaning – is the one thing that science hasn't been able to give them."

Joss responds, "Yah, yah…"

Ellie retorts, "Come on! It's like your saying science killed God. What if… what if science simply revealed that he never existed in the first place?"

After heading out to the balcony, Ellie continues attempts to disprove God.

She cites Occam's Razor named after English Franciscan friar William of Ockham (1287-1357) who was a scholastic philosopher and theologian.[11] In the movie, Ellie cites it as a scientific principle. Occam's Razor is actually a philosophical problem-solving principle.

The principle essentially states that "simpler solutions are more likely to be correct than complex ones."

Ellie asks in the middle of their conversation about the proof of existence for God, "How do you know you're not deluding yourself? Ah, for me, I'd need proof?"

Joss Palmer contemplates, "Proof."

Looking away he asks Ellie, "Did you love your father?"

Ellie reacts, "What?"

Joss repeats, "Your dad. Did you love him?"

Ellie replies, "Yes, very much."

Joss, "Prove it."

Faith Sees the Unseeable

I've watched this movie a dozen times and thought of the seeming contradictions between science and faith. Which is easier to believe:

a random occurring universe, or an architect beyond our comprehension designing it all?

Ellie put it this way, "All things being equal, the simplest explanation tends to be the right one."

For me, there's a simpler explanation with infinitesimally fewer problems compared to a Big Bang. A powerful majestic being created this ever-expanding universe out of a vast nothingness.

Sitting as a speck upon this earth – a mere speck itself – in a solar system that is but one speck in this speck of a galaxy called the Milky Way, how can one claim that all things are equal? The more we learn about what's out there, the more we learn how little we actually know about what's out there.

Is it easier to assume that this ever-vast expanding universe over billions of years collided, exploded, inflated into multi-verses of colliding banes recycling endlessly from vast nothingness to form billions of celestial bodies into a seemingly organized orbits around warm giving stars throughout millions of galaxies?[12]

Or, rather a higher intelligence created the universe of lessor intelligent beings – us – for specific purposes?

Faith Makes the Intangible Tangible

The 11th chapter of Hebrews gives the intangibles of human existence reasonableness in God. Faith is a far more tangible solution to me.

Faith is my Hubble and Kepler. For "by faith we understand that the entire universe was formed at God's command, that what we now see did not come from anything that can be seen." — Hebrews 11:3 "Impossible," you say? Prove it.

Faith Gives Meaning to the Meaningless

Hebrews chapter eleven lists twenty-two people as examples of faith. The chapter finishes, "All these people earned a good reputation because of their faith, yet none of them received all that God had promised. For God had something better in mind for us, so that they would not reach perfection without us." — Hebrews 11:39

Much of our interactions with people find those struggling to gain a sense of meaning and purpose. This is a perplexing commonality today. What is my purpose? What's meaningful? What should I give myself to?

Hebrews 11 tells me that the Westminster Catechism is correct when it claims, "Man's chief end is to glorify God, and to enjoy him forever."

Faith is the tangible that makes sensing intangibles possible. Faith is all important.

Ponderings

→ How does faith give meaning to you?

→ How does faith help you see and touch the intangibles of God?

→ Or, perhaps, how does faith fail and disappoint?

– 6 –

Faith-Strugglers

*Faith is about wanting God more than
the thing you want from God.*

— D. J. Mingo

Have you ever heard someone talk about another person's faith?

That person has deep faith.
That person's faith is weak.
Their faith is strong.
His faith helped him achieve that.
Her faith enabled her to overcome that hardship in life.

I don't doubt such accounts, but… it seems to me that… faith mostly receives credit when someone endures one of life's difficult gut punches, or a desired outcome occurs.

Faith helped them do this or that. Faith helped that person reach success. A high income level. A position in a company. A physical recovery from illness or injury.

A reporter interviewing a successful college quarterback asked, "How does your success on the football field define you?" The young talented athlete replied, "It's not football that defines me. Wins or losses. Criticisms of a bad year. Injuries and recovery during the off season. It's my faith that defines me."

Some celebrities claim faith as a key to their successes.[13] Athletes cite faith enabling them to play bigger than themselves.[14] Other noteworthy people cite faith as key to their outcomes in life.

Faith Accounts

A South African farmer once shared his story of severe loss. A storm hurled hailstones the size of golf balls upon his farm. In only a few minutes his crops laid devastated. Damage to buildings and vehicles rendered his farm incapable of producing for several years.

Listening to him share his story, a smile emerged from his wrinkled face as his blue eyes beamed. He ended, "These things do not trouble me as it does others. Faith in God gives me confidence that this is not an end but only another beginning."

A story told by a missionary serving in the jungles of Brazil in the 1960s still intrigues. A great tale of faith.

As missionaries serving in a remote part of South America, sickness proved a constant companion. Their child was struck by a high fever and battled for life in the hot jungles of the interior. Without electricity there was little they could do to help ease the child's spiking fever.

Praying for God to heal their little boy, a fierce storm broke out. Within minutes during their darkest time, a rare event occurred. The storm covered the ground with hail. They packed their precious son in hail stones to bring down his fever to help ease the infection. Faith won the day, and the hail stones too.

People experiencing healings from traumatic injuries or illnesses ascribe faith as an essential ingredient to their recoveries.

We hear these stories, but many of us struggle to relate to these examples. Faith often feels abstract. Distant and inaccessible. A talking point in church. Someone else's experience.

Such amazing tales of faith tell of another's story. Someone else's experience. Not mine. Not yours too, perhaps. For many, faith is a struggle to experience that which we claim to believe.

Sitting by the bedside of our son at Children's Hospital in Dallas, Texas a well-meaning woman offered a prayer of faith. She prayed that our faith in God might prevail to heal our son.

Daniel recovered from the ordeal. I'm not sure whether faith contributed to our son's recovery. However, gratitude marked our relief.

A talented woman in the midst of the Great Recession of 2008 faced losing her business. She whimpered, "I've prayed about this many times. Perhaps, my faith is just too weak for God to help me here." Several months later her company closed. She's never recovered from as she called it, "My devastation."

A wonderful young single woman praying for a soul mate cried, "By faith, I'm believing you, God, to bring me a caring husband." She married a man who after a few years began to physically abused her. The marriage lasted five years before she escaped to safety by divorcing him. Her faith took a direct hit leaving her bewildered with a sense of hopelessness.

A young family huddled around the bedside of their son listened to the words of a visiting friend. "If your faith is strong enough, God will heal your child."

With the loss of their child a few days later, I still remember hearing their confusion, "Was the death of our son due to some deficiency of our faith?"

Faith Camps

As a young teenage boy, mom sent us to Youth Retreats every summer with the Boys – now Boys and Girls – Club of America up in Willow River, Minnesota. At the retreat, leaders divided the boys into two camps.

One camp consisted of Order of the Athabasca. Different colored sashes – red, blue, yellow and green – worn by its members represented varying levels of wilderness skills.

Knot tying. Archery. Riflery. Boating. Horseback riding. Handling a knife and axe. Outdoor survival skills, and an array of other achievements marked an elite group of campers and counselors.

The other camp involved sashless youth. Some young boys cared nothing for the sashes. They attended the Youth Retreat only for the fun. For others it marked their first summer to attend.

Then, there was a third camp. A group of teenage boys who failed at every attempt to obtain a sash. They didn't tie knots well. Their arrows missed targets. Their riflery skills kept them out of the running. Regardless of how often they attempted to earn a sash, they failed.

Those camps remind me of people today who talk about faith. They make up different faith camps. People who experience varying degrees of faith satisfaction.

Faith Elites Camp marks a group of people with often-amazing stories to tell. Faith celebrities proclaim themselves as examples to follow. We celebrate them rehearsing their stories. Theirs is the stuff that books are written about. Podcasts focus upon. Faith stories of success and emulation.

Faith Expressionists Camp finds a faith that addresses every aspect of life. Faith grants the ability to deal with any challenge. From finding a parking spot in a crowded downtown city to getting a job, faith is there.

A decision to purchase a truck – or bottle of orange juice for that matter – marks a faith venture.

People of this camp talk proudly of faith wearing their words with pride. Faith explains all their successes because of a seed of faith they sowed obligating God to increase their possessions and stations of life.

Faith Etymologist Camp. An etymologist is a word expert, particularly the history of words and their origins. Faith etymologists like to talk and teach much about the meaning of "faith."

Faith here often slides towards an intellectual ascent of a narrowly defined belief. A lesson to teach. A biblical concept to exegete. A sermon to preach.

"Only by faith," does one gain entrance into heaven. This is a key teaching of most evangelical churches. But, beyond an initial consideration of a salvation decision, faith doesn't seem to bare much practical influence. Faith feels predestine or fatalistic.

Faith becomes more about what you believe and less about what you do with it.

Which Faith Camp? One side of the faith spectrum roots itself in experience. Touch faith. Feel faith. Experience faith. Faith conquers addictions, obesity, marital strife, economic turmoil, and the list goes on. Numerous expounders of faith cite this approach when raising funds for their causes through "A Seed of Faith" teaching.

To them, strong faith aligns with successful, healthy, beautiful, athletic and wealthy – especially the latter – people. This view is not limited to only American Christianity. Traveling the world, I see such teachings in the most impoverished of communities.

I'm not insinuating that this type of faith doesn't exist in such experiences. However, my years in Africa as a missionary witnessed a richness of faith among poor sickly people rarely seen here in the West.

Faith in death. Faith in life. Faith in loss. Faith in hardship. Faith in celebration. Faith in sickness. Faith in suffering. Not just faith in prosperity.

We read little about minimum wage earners being people of faith. Or subsistence third-world people exhibiting much faith. People with faith don't struggle to find food to support their families. Right?

The oncology waiting room finds few authors looking to interview people of faith. Sick dying people don't possess much faith. Or, do they?

Don't think you'll find many looking for people of faith among PTSD sufferers. Faith doesn't dwell among the mentally ill. Right?

Then, the other side of faith seems expressionless. Though acknowledged, it's the stuff of liturgy and lessons. It states a confidence that is grounded in biblical truth. It defines faith as foundational to belief.

Don the Doubter

There is – I think – another camp of people to consider. The largest camp, perhaps. A camp caught in the middle of two faith opposites. A pragmatic depiction of people trying to figure out real faith. These are Faith-strugglers.

Faith-strugglers represent – I suspect – most of us. Those hearing of faith, believing in faith, seeing its necessity, but yet struggling to see any practical benefit from it. They may agree that the righteous must live by faith, but faith meagerly survives from day to day.

The Bible is loaded with faith-strugglers. I like the Apostle Thomas. I think he's the kind of person I'd relate to over a cup of coffee. He's a guy who lived with Jesus for almost 3 years. When Christ appeared to his disciples after his death, Thomas doubted that Christ actually stood before him.

Jesus said to Thomas, "Put your finger here, and look at my hands. Put your hand into the wound in my side. Don't be faithless any longer. Believe!" — John 20:27

It marked a wonderful moment. Jesus reaching out to Thomas helping him in his faith-struggle. That's what I love about Jesus. After all that Christ went through, here he was lovingly challenging Thomas to believe rather than criticizing him for his doubts.

How is Thomas remembered for that exchange? Rather than Thomas the Jesus-follower, he's named, Thomas the Doubter. Typical of people – you and me – to see only the negative.

When it comes to seeing God in every aspect of our lives, most of us are doubters. We all lean towards Thomas.

Don the Doubter describes many of my interactions between life and faith. It does me well to think of a lovingly patient Jesus encouraging me to take a next small faith-step forward rather than a faith shamer blasting me for my lack of it.

Faith is a struggle not because it's hard, but because it's easy. Simply believe. It's the object of our belief that makes faith a struggle. Not so much how we believe, but in what we believe in.

Faith or doubt. There's little in between.

Ponderings

→ Which faith camp do you belong to?

→ What's your greatest faith experience?

→ What about your faith disappointments?

→ How do you struggle with your faith?

– 7 –

Faith Conundrums

Usually, the main problem with life conundrums is that we don't bring to them enough imagination.

— Thomas Moore

Relying on God has to begin all over again every day as if nothing had yet been done.

— C. S. Lewis

Another faith account stands out during my years in Africa. Des – a South African – often spoke with me about faith. I guess being a missionary and all, Des perhaps thought that challenging me on faith might clarify the subject for him.

Once he said, "You know I have a friend. Their baby died, but they have strong faith. They tell me, 'We trust everything to God.'"

He concluded with, "Faith, I just don't get it. It's all a conundrum to me."

Des's words characterizes many faith conundrums:

I tried faith, but it doesn't seem to deliver as promised.

My child still died.
I'm still not happy.
He/she still left me.
My children won't talk to me.
I still got hurt.
My marriage still failed.
They violated me.
He used me.
She cheated on me.
They eliminated my job.
The church didn't appreciate me.
Prayer is empty.

Faith – well – it seems real, but it doesn't work for me.

Faith sometimes can present more of a conundrum than a comfort. Conundrums – challenges – find many giving up. However, I submit that a conundrum of life is not a reason to abandon a certain thing but rather to approach it, wrestle with it, and gain from it.

Faith Icons

Once a young woman visiting me in my office exclaimed, "Ok, I read the whole Bible. I don't see anything that relates to me and my situation. All those people mentioned in the Bible are like heroes. They're not like us today."

As a single mom, working two jobs, going to night school, and raising two children, she believed no one in the Bible related to her situation. Until we looked at the prophet Samuel's mother, Hannah.

Hannah's simple faith was, "God give me a man child and I will give him back to you." Hannah's faith pleased God. In return, God pleased Hannah with a son. A child that shaped the future of Israel.

As we discussed Hannah, the single mom blurted out, "Oh, faith is like that?" Laughing I replied, "Well, yes, I suppose so." She replied, "Well, I can do that!"

As we read the Bible, it's easy to feel that the faith mentioned in Scripture is that of superheroes. Not me. Not you. More like unrelatable icons out of touch with us in this life.

Faith Show-and-Tell

Listening to others' accounts of their faith-experiences can prove defeating too. Hearing faith journeys of present-day authors, leaders, and Christian speakers tends to put faith on a top shelf out of reach for most of us.

We become hearers of other's faith but not genuine possessors of our own. We talk of another's faith experience, but a question stymies us, "What does my faith do for me?"

When Faith Doesn't Work

"You don't have enough faith," Jesus told them. "I tell you the truth, if you had faith even as small as a mustard seed, you could say to this mountain, 'Move from here to there,' and it would move. Nothing would be impossible." — (Matthew 17:20)

A hundred if not a thousand times I questioned the quality of my faith. Torturing myself with self-accusations of infantile faith led me down a path of frustration.

I believed in faith. I believed in God. I believed I put my faith in God. But, I also believed that for some reason my faith didn't work efficiently. When that occurred, every consideration showed the object of my faith was something other than God. That's when I discovered that faith is only as strong as its object.

With faith, I sought to stymie PTSD's nightmares. The depression. Disturbed nights seeing less than three hours sleep. A startling which rocked my inner world every time a door slammed, a bang occurred, or a set of keys dropped onto a ceramic floor.

"This is my fault," I thought, "A lack of faith. You're such a hypocrite. Give it up. Withdraw to some cave somewhere. Faith will not help you here."

My faith seemed too small. Faith reaching high enough to overcome consequences of the past, and actions of the present didn't appear to exist.

Then, another thought. Maybe my faith is not real? The whole believe in God thing is one big hoax. Sincere people believing sincerely in something that is out of reach.

Yet, faith did work. Sometimes.

Faith overcame anger at the mere mention of a derelict father.

It disabled scars left by an alcoholic mother who – when surrendered to booze – turned from a nurturing mother into an assaulting aggressor.

Faith came alongside dozens of terminally dying African children in our care centers in South Africa. Children often perishing due to nothing more than the flu. An illness that simple medicine available in the West might easily cure. Poverty put much of that out of reach for poor grieving parents.

Faith did in fact offer solace for many traumatic episodes both past and present in my life.

Yet, recalling many episodes as a kid in North Minneapolis, Minnesota, the experience of holding an African child in my arms dying of AIDS, or the soul searing event of seeing four Zulu men burned alive just because of their political affiliation caused my

Faith to wane as those experiences played repeatedly in my mind.
To retreat into the back woods of my soul.
To go into hiding.
To barely creep along.

A Shoe Box of Faith

Recently, I went through an old shoebox my mother left me before she died. In it was my baptismal certificate. In my first moments of life, my baptism made me a member of the Roman Catholic Church.

Sixteen years later, putting my faith in Jesus Christ alone – a moment of decision – granted me membership into a Baptist church along with another baptism.

In both cases, faith seemed more of a guarantee, an assurance of the next life rather than a guide in this life.

Faith In Africa

During my many years in Southern Africa, many wonderful people shared their faith.

Hindus talked of faith in their Scriptures, Vedas and Upanishads, the ultimate reality – Brahman – and the interconnection of humans with the universe.

A Muslim businessman once gifted me with a Quran. We talked about Islam's Pillars of Faith, the Oneness of God, the messengers and prophets. Muslims unwavering faith in Allah impressed me.

44

Zulus often spoke of their ancestral heritage and manner of respect offered to family members no longer living. Early missionaries often labeled the practice as, "Ancestor Worship." However, "respect" became my preferred word.

Traditional Zulus respect their ancestors. They talk with them often asking for help and favor to navigate the challenges of life. In this, many Zulus put their faith in departed family members.

The people of this world showed me that faith is an innermost private and special connection of all experiences. The common element that binds humans together. All practices believes in something.

My travels throughout the world sees many beautiful people of sincere practicing faith. People directing their faith towards something. A perceived betterness. A higher way. A creator.

Conundrums of faith also presented themselves in almost every conversation about faith. Often, followers of other religions expressed a hint of dissatisfaction in what they believed. An, "I'm not quite sure who this really helps me right now."

Outside of a foundational belief about their faith, few shared any underpinnings of how that faith benefited them in any practical function of daily life.

Ponderings

→ What faith conundrums are you experiencing?

→ To What/whom do you look to in faith? Yes, God, and what else?

– 8 –

Faith's Indirect Objects

Faith is the art of holding on to things your reason has once accepted in spite of your changing moods.

— C. S. Lewis

Let's look at English grammar. Who really enjoyed studying grammar in school? Yet, English grammar taught me many important principles.

In grammar, we learned that an indirect object is the person or thing that receives the effect of the action of a verb with two objects.[15]

An example is, "He gave me the book." The direct object is "book" and the indirect object is "me."[16]

Another example, "Jeff threw Mark the ball." Jeff is the subject. What did Jeff throw? The <u>ball</u>. Ball is the **direct object**. Who received the ball? Mark. <u>Mark</u> is the indirect object.[17]

When I examined my past faith endeavors, it brought a troubling realization. Faith often centered more upon me than God. Faith in what I wanted from God became more about me and less about God. This put me as the direct object of my faith. God became secondary as my prayers slotted God into an indirect object of faith.

This is faith's great weakness.
The reason faith doesn't seem to work.
When faith becomes more about us
– what we want – and less about God.

What I needed, wanted, or desired for others often stepped in front of God. What I wanted became my faith's direct object. Faith's want rather than faith's worship. Faith too often looked like this for me:

Faith ⟶ needs, wants, desires = God

Faith's experiences consisted little of God, and much about myself. My prayer lists. My needs. My wants. My desires. Faith too often meant getting what I wanted from God more than getting close to God.

Faith Follies

Let's take a pastor for instance. The pastor prays fervently that God will increase the number of attenders in the church. What is the actual motive for an increase in attendance?

As a young believer – only 16 years old – our pastor encouraged us to trust God for 300 people to attend a special Sunday. For many weeks, prayers went before God.

He exhorted, "Count it as true and it will be so." On that special Sunday, 258 people attended.

Another pastor once grumbled at me, "I'm mad with God because no matter what I do my church is small." There's a host of spiritual deficits in that statement. After eighteen years of pastoring, he resigned citing his anger with God for not answering his prayer.

What about a missionary praying God will help them raise money for their family or ministry?

Or, a faith community struggling financially asking God to help pay off the mortgage on their facility. The church I'm thinking of while writing this sentence actually closed.

What about the lonely person praying for friends?

Or, the couple begging God for fertility so a child can grace their home?

A business owner asking God to help build a successful company?

That person praying for healing and wholeness?

A person praying – not making this up – for a winning lottery ticket, promising generosity in return. No joke. The first church I worked in as a young intern staff member told of his prayer for God to give him a winning lottery ticket.

He went around telling everyone that a huge sum of money was coming his way promising everyone help with their financial struggles. And, so much could be done for the kingdom of God! As if God needed a winning lottery ticket's winnings.

He never won. You've got a better chance of waking up in the morning and stubbing your toe on a bag of gold getting out of bed than buying a jackpot lottery ticket. Sounds pathetic?

We sort of do this all the time. Don't we?

Fill in your blank. I am trusting by faith that God gives / helps me to

_____?

49

Please hear me out – I'm not stating that praying for any of these things is wrong. Well, maybe a winning lottery ticket is a bit of a stretch. My thoughts center around the question, "What constitutes faith?"

The answer I've come to is:

Faith is defined by its object: its greatest want.

Misaligned Objects of Faith

When faith is directed towards God for only the purpose of acquiring or succeeding, then desire becomes the object of faith. God becomes the indirect object as a means to get what we want.

An honest contemplation of my past faith practices discovered that God entered my faith equations somewhere in the middle. Between the subject of me and the direct object of what I wanted. Sadly, brutal honesty indicated God was not the first priority of my faith. Often, not even close.

Paying close attention to the many prayers uttered in church, Bible studies, and small groups reinforces that my struggle is not unique.

Many prayers center upon good and religious things. Upon health, finances and wellness. A thing to acquire. A friendship to kindle. Or, a career to succeed at.

While all of these desired acquisitions points towards a better life, they replace God as faith's object. God is relegated to a lessor importance in faith. Indirect because our wants can easily supersede God in our souls and minds.

Here's the real danger of it all. Anything valued above God engenders the development of idols in our lives.

Just like the idols in the Old Testament that people created with their own hands only to bow down and worship, so too can our attainments become idols when placed before God.

Making God of secondary importance – an indirect object – of faith resembles:

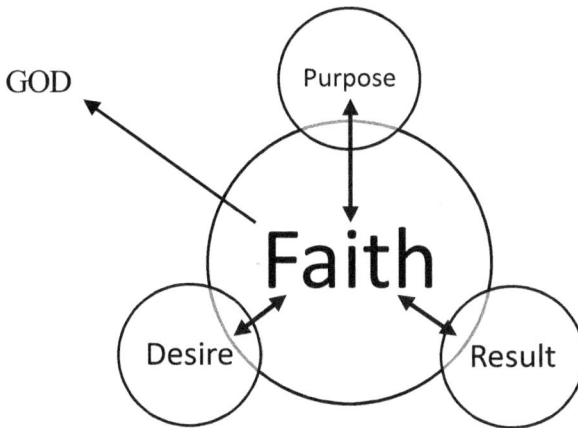

Ponderings

Write down any indirect objects of your faith. Be honest. Think about it. Come on now…

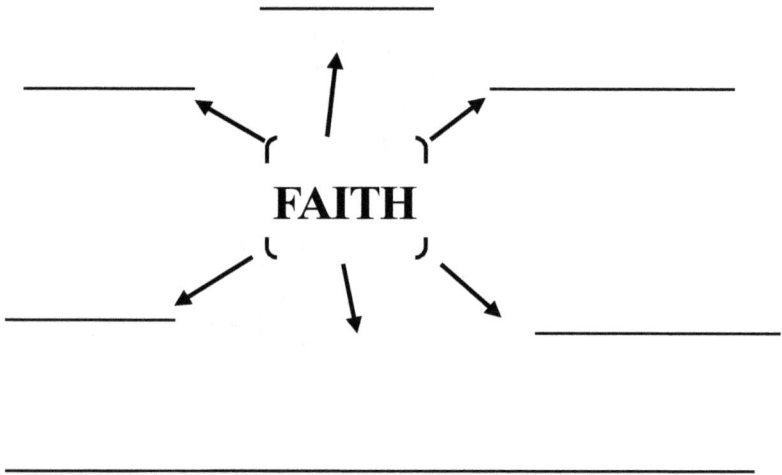

$$\text{FAITH}$$

_____

_____ _____

_____ _____

_____

– 9 –

When Faith Becomes

Its Own Idol

There are times when faith worships faith more than pursues God. Well-meaning spiritually inquisitive people who believe their faith brings them closer to God, when perhaps… it actually drives them further from God.

One says, "I have faith."

Faith in what? For what? To what end?

Can't tell you how many times good church attenders looked at me with shrugged shoulders and bewilderment to such questions. I'm not critical of them. I've been there myself.

Faith seems to worship faith:

**When faith makes God anything else
but its sole object.**

When we worship faith for faith's sake, we possess faith just for the sake of faith. Faith becomes little more than a trinket. Our good luck charm. A bargaining chip with God to promote ourselves. Or, a life preserver when life's troubles throw us off the decks of our confidence into stormy waters.

When anything else but God becomes faith's first objective, then faith – not God – can become a god. Something bowed before in soul, and worshiped other than God.

God, I'm putting my faith in you for that new job.
For that new car, God.
To help my marriage.
For that winning lottery ticket.
For prosperity and success.
For happiness.
For health.
For acceptance.
For a big church.
Influential ministry.
God, I'm trusting you to bring in the money to pay off my student loans.
God, I'm trusting you that my expectation for life will be…
For my book to become a best seller.
For this or that all IN YOUR NAME! It's all for you God!
For, for, for…

What is the difference between a person's faith that God responds to and another's faith who experiences unanswered prayers?

The answer is faith's object. *Faith is no stronger than its most direct object.* This presents us with our most important consideration.

What is the object/s of your faith?

"I asked God to help me acquire this, accomplished that, or become this," marked my thinking. Only danger with this thinking is it pulls us away from the Greatest Commandment:

The man answered, 'You must love the LORD your God with all your heart, all your soul, all your strength, and all your mind.'

— Luke 10:27

Conceited Faith

Let's look at an indirect object again. Remember, an indirect object tells what or for whom something is done. The indirect object always comes between the verb and the direct object."[18]

Let's apply this to faith:

"I'm trusting God to make **me** successful in my business."

Who is the subject of this faith? "I" is the subject. The direct object appears to be God, but it actually centers upon "me." See the focus of this faith attempt? It's more a prayer of self, desiring something more for self, pushing God off to the side. I present we unknowingly do this all the time.

This is a critical faith-flaw. When faith focuses upon other than God, faith's object becomes lessor and weak. When this happens, worship centers upon something other than God. The Bible calls this idolatry. Just as idolatrous as those people in the Old Testament who bowed before a golden calf in Exodus.

When we do this, faith centers upon other than the Creator. Is this the reason why our prayers at times are so ineffective and disappointing? *God is not real, because faith is not focused upon Him.* When faith leads people away from God – even though in the name of God – and to themselves, then faith replaces God with itself.

Strong faith centers itself in God.

Faith possesses no more power than the objects we trust to it. And, faith solely for faith's sake places faith as its own object. This kind of faith – I fear so prevalent today – can lead to a dry barren wasteland of religion.

Consumerism Faith

When approaching God as only a means of receiving what I need, want, or feel, is that faith at all? To me. this resembles more of standing in line at Walmart waiting to pay for the goods in my cart.

If faith is only about my prosperity, my health, my happiness or station of life, then faith becomes little more than a religious commodity. An item placed in a faith cart pushed up and down the aisles of religious experiences.

Plenty of these type of faith proclaimers use Scripture to support their thinking. "Ask and ye shall receive!" Or, "Ask anything in Jesus' name!" Yes, this is true, but the emphasis here is upon Jesus not what a person chooses.

At the Faith Walmart Store, our want-things appear on the faith shelves in front of you. Our faith cards allows us to take anything we desire. Take it! The more we use our faith cards the more faith points we accrue.

Gaining faith points grants access to bigger warehouses. Like a game show host you suddenly hear, "It's A NEW CAR!" Now, god becomes a new car.

Faith is the key. Get faith and you'll get stuff.

There's also a department of happiness. That's right. Gaining enough faith points on your faith card grants you happiness.

Acquiring faith points occurs in many ways. Believe. Give. Attend. Affirm. The more you do for more faith, the more points you accrue. Prevalent preaching today teaches that faith is a force you can use to get what you want from God.[19]

Faith is the membership card you show when entering the faith-warehouse of wants. Sort of Sam's Club or a Costco.

However, simply pushing your faith cart up and down the isles only to grab what you want is not faith. And, I don't think God much cares for it.

God slips out from our soul's view as we crowd our carts with garnishments and products; everything except God.

Perhaps this is exactly what Jesus talked about when facing a hostile religious crowd as he quoted from the Old Testament in Isaiah 29:13:

'These people honor me with their lips, but their hearts are far from me. Their worship is a farce, for they teach man-made ideas as commands from God.'

Faith Like Grandparents

Grandparents almost physically force me at times to view – how do I say this? – um, they're not so always beautiful grandchildren.

How many times has someone forced you to look at a photo of someone's baby and you thought, "Ah… ok." Grandparents are egregious offenders here.

Every grandparent believes their grandkidos gorgeous above all else. More talented than Beethoven. Smarter than Einstein. A gifted child above all others. A new grandparent armed with a smartphone is a dangerous thing. Let me tell you.

I once contemplated the movie *The Last Samurai* where towards the end of the movie Captain Nathan Algren – played by Tom Cruise – helps Ken Watanabe, playing Katsumoto, commit Seppuku by jamming his knife – tantō – deep into his gut.

As a grandma swiped to the umpteenth picture on the phone of her runny nosed grandkid, my imagination found me on the battlefield looking for Nathan Algren with a tantō to end my suffering.

Besides, I've got 15 beautiful grandkidos, which by the way, trumps your grandchildren anyways any day.

I think faith is like this sometimes. Faith itself is not something one can show. It's an intangible. Invisible. Yet, faith is a spiritual picture of sorts. It's not the faith itself, but the results of faith that presents an image or concept to admire, talk about and share.

Faith's Reboot Loop

Once I owned a computer that just kept rebooting. Regardless of how many times I pushed the power button, the dumb thing restarted repeatedly.

Upon taking it to a computer guru friend he quickly ascertained the problem. He explained that the computer suffered from something on the hard drive causing a reboot loop. The computer busied itself trying to function accomplishing nothing but continually restarting.

As I understood it, the computer's hard drive focused upon other programs in the startup. Rather than connecting to the BIOS – Basic Input/Output System – the system chased other programs loaded on the hard drive. Once redirected to focus upon the BIOS, my computer booted up again.

Faith is like that. When praying, contemplating, or talking with God, often our faith wanders away from the Logos. — John 1:1

Faith is no more powerful than the object of its trust.[20] If faith becomes faith's own object, then faith looks to faith only. A faith reboot loop occurs. Possessing no object to direct it towards, faith recycles itself in itself. Faith fails to flourish going no further than itself.

God as faith's only object is the kind of faith that gains God's attention. In gaining his attention, God's compensations follow surpassing our self-centered desires. It is here that God answers our prayers, when faith's object is stronger than faith itself.

Then, what God gives us is better than what we originally wanted for ourselves because our wants are now centered in God.

Ponderings

→ Who or what receives the action of your faith?

Faith ⟶

→ Has faith become an idol?

→ What might you do to make God the object of your faith?

– 10 –

So, What Is Faith and How Do I Get It?

We are what we believe we are.

— C. S. Lewis

If the words written about faith became drops of water, the land masses of this earth might disappear under the many words written about it. What else can exist to say about faith? Yet, many people struggle to answer this question? "What is faith?"

An easy answer is,

Faith is believing with certainty in something that seems or feels uncertain.

Someone once pressed me, "Are you certain that God exists?" I replied, "Yes, quite certain." The person pushed me again, "How can you be certain in that which is so uncertain?" "Certain" to him was being able to see, touch or experience.

Then he went for his rehearsed knockout blow, "Well, certainly you can't see God, so it's impossible to believe in God with any amount of certainty." He really liked the word "certainty."

The conversation ended abruptly as I replied, "Of the uncertainty of you which you speak, I am confident that that uncertainty certainly exists beyond any uncertainty. At least certainly for me." He grunted as he made his way to the door.

Faith's Ratio

*You don't have enough faith, I tell you the truth, if you had **faith even as small as a mustard seed**, you could say to this mountain, 'Move from here to there,' and it would move. Nothing would be impossible.*

— Matthew 17:20

According to Jesus, any amount of legitimate faith is compensated. Jesus' words here show that faith is quantifiable. Even small faith is acknowledged and receives a response from God. Faith waits for an uncovering by its holder.

Faith's People

Faith is not reserved for only champions and heroes. For only those of deepest piety and resolve. Real faith is the domain of real people like you and me.

Here's some great news. It doesn't take a lot of faith to get God's attention. Just a little works!

There are quite a few unsung people of faith in the Bible. Names rarely mentioned who experienced great results because of their faith.

Hannah, a real mom. — 1 Samuel 1 & 2

Rahab, a real woman caught in a cycle of desperation. — Joshua 2:9-13

A Real solider, just doing his job. — Matthew 8:5-13

Or, a single mom struggling to survive and support her son. — 1 Kings 17

Real people like you and me.

What makes God real is that a relative nobody – like me – can through faith experience His goodness. Not only believe in this goodness, but actually live and breathe it.

My favorite explanation of faith comes from the book of Hebrews in the New Testament. In Chapter 11 of the first verse, faith is explained.

Faith shows the reality of what we hope for;
it is the evidence of things we cannot see.

The reality of what we hope for; the evidence of things we cannot see.

Reality ⟶ hope
Evidence ⟶ the unseen

"Reality" – "The state of things as they actually exist, as opposed to an idealistic or notional idea of them."[21]

"Hope" – "A feeling of expectation and desire for a particular thing to happen."[22]

"Evidence" – "The available body of facts or information indicating whether a belief or proposition is true or valid."[23]

"Unseen" – "Not seen or noticed."[24]

Hope and reality. Evidence and unseen. Mysterious paradoxes of faith. Hoping in a reality not yet seen. Hum...

I like English Romantic Poet William Woodsworth impression of faith, ***"Faith is a passionate intuition."***

That's what I'm looking for.

A passionate intuition that God is real in my life.

An intuition of connection.

A sense of something that exists yet does not yet fully appear.

An obsessive awareness of an occurrence.

Something or someone that brings a betterment to my faith.

Reentering a deep mine shaft of faith in the book of Hebrews, an often-explored old vein of truth reappeared. Observing, looking and studying the verse from a hundred angles, dozens of translations, and in several languages, a rich faith-vein of ore appeared:

Now faith is the **substance** of things hoped for, the evidence of things not seen.

— Hebrews 11:1 (KJV)

Faith's Awareness

If you could hold faith in your hand what might it look like? Note the word "substance." Faith is the **substance** of what we hope for. The nitty gritty of it all.

As substance, faith makes hope tangible; spiritually measurable.

Once I heard a man suffering from a spinal cord injury (SCI) say during an interview, "There is great hope in the SCI community."

Hope is palpable. Faith makes it so.

The word "substance" here in Hebrews 11:1 is deeper than a glance might indicate. The author in the language he wrote the book used the word "hypostasis." It is a word still used in English today.

Hypostasis comes from two words in the Greek language. "Hupo" meaning "under." And, "statsis" meaning "standing." Putting both words together form the Greek word "hupostasis." Hupostasis carries the idea of sediment and foundation.[25] Or, simply understanding.

Through the centuries with the influence of Latin the word developed into hypostasis. Regarding faith, it carries the idea of something which actually exists.

Faith is real.
Faith is substantive.
Faith is practical.
Faith connects the soul's experiences to God.

Several years of journaling during my darkest hours of PTSD, led to a personal discovery. My own words asked, "Faith in what? Faith in who? Faith to what end? Towards what goal? To what accomplishments?" As a young inquisitor once pressed me, "Faith, what's in it for me?"

Whatever the order, it seems – according to Jesus – we don't need a lot of faith to enjoy faith's benefits. And, the key to unlocking faith is found in 4 secrets clearly revealed in one verse in the Bible.

The 4 Secrets to Faith Principle lie in this one verse:

¹But without faith it is impossible to please Him,
²for he who comes to God
³must believe that He is,
and that
⁴He is a rewarder of those who diligently seek Him.

— Hebrews 11:6 (KJV)

In this verse lies the 4 secrets of a personal satisfying sustainable faith. Particularly, in the last sentence. He is a rewarder, compensator and recompenser of those who diligently – persistently – seek Him.

Faith then is a coming to God – in certainty and sincerity – believing that God compensates those who spend their energies and time wanting Him.

Ponderings

→ What does your faith really want?

– 11 –

Faith's Direct Object

To one who has faith, no explanation is necessary. To one without faith, no explanation is possible.

— Thomas Aquinas

What does faith look towards? What is faith's focus? Its desire? Its pleasure? Its purpose?

I love the comic strip *Dilbert* by Scott Adams. When talking with his anthropomorphic dog he cites, "… and we know mass creates gravity because dense planets have more gravity." His dog – Dogbert – asks, "How do we know which planets are more dense?" Dilbert answers, "They have more gravity." Dogbert replies, "That's circular reasoning." Dilbert ends, "I prefer to think of it as having no loose ends."[26]

Sometimes our faith resembles circular reasoning, I'm afraid. One might say, "I have faith because I believe. Another says, "I believe because I possess faith."

Before looking at *4 Secrets to Making Your Faith Work Again,* there's a foundational principle that determines whether faith is worth anything at all. To me, it's the bedrock of working faith.

It's the reason I've waited until the middle of this book to reveal its 4 secrets. The Faith Principle pivots on this one principle:

God is the sole object of faith.

Observation is one principle of Bible interpretation. As such, we look at Hebrews 11:6 again from a different angle. It emphasizes that faith's object is solely and only God. God as faith's object is **emphasized 5 times** in this verse:

*And it is impossible to please **God** without faith. Anyone who wants to <u>come</u> to **him** must <u>believe</u> that **God** exists and that **he** rewards those who sincerely <u>seek</u> **him.***

— Emphasis mine

Faith's Source

"Anyone who wants to come to him..." What faith wants, seeks, and desires above all other considerations is God.

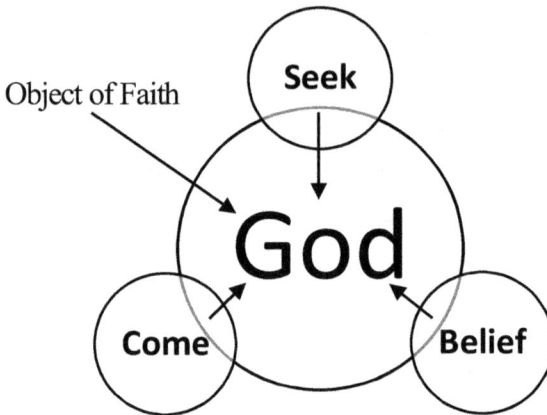

Object of Faith

Seek

God

Come

Belief

The object of our faith determines its true North. When Faith's object is God, faith works. When faith's object is lesser than God it struggles.

A brief perusal of popular books in the Christian market today cites many examples of faith. A faith that produced success. Her faith brought fame. His faith helped him overcome. Their faith in God brought them...

In many Christian books – success, fame, health and are the objects of faith. That's why people buy the book as they ponder, "Faith, what's in it for me?"

Faith then attaches God to a result or station of life rather than to our relationship with God. God ceases as the focus becoming only a means to acquire.

To me, this kind of faith looks like this:

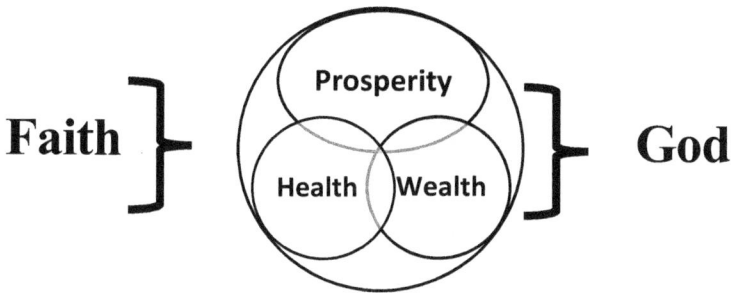

Often, the three letters G-O-D are added into the mix. However, this is not the kind of faith God rewards because its motivation directs faith away from God towards something or someone other than God.

This puts our wants as the object of faith's desire. This faith objectifies God as only part of faith rather than its purest essence.

Many times our faith struggles because of an underlying, unrealized, and undeclared spiritual narcissism: what we really want from faith is more of a focus upon ourselves.

Faith Looks Towards God First

God – and God only – must become faith's object. The God of the universe, not just the gods of the what I aspire to attain or become. A faith that clings to the certainty of God.

Have you ever given someone something special? A gift? A surprise? Then, as your magnanimous gesture fades into memory you're forgotten about or pushed aside for something or someone else? It's perhaps at that point, you discovered that the object of your friendship was more about what your friend received from you rather than you yourself.

Yes, God gives – rewards – stuff, but the stuff we receive from God is not the object of faith. God is. God rewards us sometimes with good health, but health itself is not the object of our faith: God is. God rewards us with relationships, but those relationships are not the object of our faith; God is.

Think about this question, "What is the center of your faith?"

The center of your attention? The easy answer for church goers is, "God," but is this a true reflection of the soul?

There's no fault in the statement itself. The challenge is in the authenticity and accuracy of such a statement compared to personal experience.

Is God – only God – truly the center of your faith?

Faith's exclusivity – from my observations – is little mentioned in the generic language of the church-faith community these days. Spiritual pragmatism and rationalism often finds faith's identity in a person's individuality rather than God.

While individuality is unique, God must mark faith's object for believing, receiving and belonging, not our personalities.

In my mid-fifties with apprehension, my That Day hobbled in my first steps. Contemplating the "how" of stepping forward in faith required giving up what I loved – our yellow white trimmed house in the woods.

After twenty-two years of missionary service in Africa, I'd earned it. A quiet life. A nice house. My little boat. Days of finishing on great grandpa's lake only 30 minutes away. Getting lost in the woods with my camera, journal and ink. A rest from my constant struggles of reliving some horrific scenes witnessed in Africa.

Yet, struggling missionaries out on their fields needed battled tested missionary survivors to help them along. Someone to say, "It's ok to hurt. It's ok to feel this way." Then ask, "How can we help you move forward?"

Hesitantly I thought, "Missionary life again? Was I out of my mind?"

The tiresome travel. The rigors of support raising. Hours driving and sitting in a car. Living out of suitcases. Noisy hotels. Staying with families who had cats. Allergies. Noise. Abandoning that which I most appreciated in the woods – silence.

Then, a bigger question arose, "What would our missionary redeployment look like?" Obstacles laid before us. Its inconveniences. The insecurities. My age. The crowded field of talented fund-raising missionaries possessing youth and vitality over a worn-out old guy like me.

One little sentence in a verse from the Bible stood up and waved at me from the pages of Scripture. Well, more like it poked me in the eye. Words read hundreds of times. Words I taught and preached.

This one little verse whispered, "Here's your answer!" It provided my faith the rudder needed to guide us towards our unknown upcoming journey.

He is a rewarder of those who diligently seek Him…

— Hebrews 11:6 KJV

Faith in a Tree

Once a friend struggling with an addiction told me about his "new faith." He chose to put his faith in a tree in his front yard to help him overcome his addiction.

I'm not making this up. Nor, am I criticizing his attempts to deal with his addiction. Or, his beliefs for that matter.

In his group therapy, the leader encouraged every person to put their faith in god as they understood it. Since he believed plants and animals to possess souls, God existed within his tree in the front yard.

He made a remarkable recovery in dealing with his addiction. Then one day he noticed the tree drooping. A close examination of the bark and leaves showed the tree sick and dying. A year later the tree was cut down. As the tree came down, so did faith as he slid back into his addiction. An addiction that later took his life.

Faith in a Church

As a little boy at the church my grandparents attended, I received First Communion and was Confirmed. That church doesn't exist anymore. The denomination in which that church existed is currently rocked with scandals and stories of abuse.

In my teens, I attended a Baptist church. Invited by a friend, I joined this church. Infighting, division, and strife destroyed the church. It doesn't exist any longer either.

Over the years, I've learned not to put my faith in churches. That kind of faith casts too high an expectation though I still attend, participate and enjoy its community. But, making a church the object of faith is not wise. Expectations tend to rise to unhealthy levels. When a hope or need is not met, faith takes a direct hit because faith focused itself upon other than God.

The landscapes of my life witnesses troupes of wounded souls wandering away from the church, faith and God. Their departures occurred through what they deemed the failure of the Church. Actually – from my perspective – it's more a failure of themselves. The failure of people. Failure of me. Failure of you. A failure of us all. Most of all, a failure of faith.

Faith in an Expectation

My friend worked for forty years for the same company. Nearing an early retirement at fifty-five, he spoke of all the wonderful things he'd planned. Sitting together in Lithonia, Georgia over lunch, we discussed his upcoming trip to teach in our Bible Institute in South Africa.

Two months after his retirement – not feeling well – he visited the doctor. Later that month he was diagnosed with stage four Pancreatic Cancer. He died less than a year after his retirement.

I suppose in the many disappointments others share with me; "expectation" is the most accurate word to describe many faith letdowns.

"It wasn't like I'd thought it be."
"My spouse…"
"That job…"
"That person…"
"That result…"
"My career path…"
"My friend…"

"The nonprofit that asked me to partner with them…"

"It just wasn't like…"

Expectations is perhaps the idol of us all.

Faith in a Company

I remember standing in the lobby of the church foyer talking to a man visiting that morning. The year was 2007. As we struck up a conversation, I asked, "Where do you work?" He replied, "Lehman Brothers." He talked fondly of the company, his career and future.

Then the Great Recession of 2008 occurred. His family – members of our church – told of how their brother lost everything. He had to start all over again in his late thirties.

A few years later, sources revealed the Target Corporation Data Breach in 2013. Within a year, every member in the church I pastored who worked for Target was forced to relocate or find other careers. Regular customers of the bullseye logo found other retailers as sales plummeted. Expectations dashed themselves upon the rocks of economic realities.

Faith in…

All of us can count examples of faith in something or someone that failed. Let us down. Someone once trusted. A person once loved. If we're honest, we might see our own failures which left people disappointed in us too.

Once in a coffee shop – overhearing a conversation at an adjacent table – a woman cried, "I'm really disappointed in him. I thought he was soooo… much better than that."

When a friend fails, faith fails if you put your faith in that friend alone. A company layoff, and faith fails. A church you vested your life into no longer wants or needs you. Faith fails. A friend betrays.

Health falters. Finances crumble. These defective objects of faith will often lead to miserable bitter producing disappointments.

Faith is only as strong as the object it's directed towards. Strong faith must secure itself in a steadfast resolute source.

That source is God.

Everyone has faith. Faith in something. Faith in someone. In an idea. A way of life. Faith – however – is only as strong at the object receiving that faith.

That Day coupled with a newfound faith marked our way forward. Looking into my soul required clearing out poor objects obstructing faith's way forward.

An honest look into my soul brought me to a rather dismal conclusion. My objects of faith often led me to a cul-de-sac of self rather than God.

The question wasn't whether I believed in God. That was a given. My faith statement started like the Apostle's Creed, "I believe in God…"

Yes, I believed in God. But as with many – I suspect – God got lost somewhere in what personal faith claimed to believe and what faith wanted. Faith got lost in faith itself.

The heart of the matter asked, "What is the object of my faith?" The first answer jumped out like a child at Vacation Bible School when raising a hand to shout out, "God!"

That's the correct answer. God for faith. God in salvation. God for heaven. But, with living – experience – what did I most often look to and trust in? Desire, destination, finance, status, health often overtook any desire for God. With close personal reflection and grim admittance, God often stood somewhere outside of what my faith claimed to value.

A redirection of faith grasped at a new perspective written in the pages of my journal,

God is the sole object of my faith.

I purposed to seek God above all else in our next steps. Whatever lay before us, God was first priority.

Seek the Kingdom of God above all else,
and live righteously,
and he will give you everything you need.

Jesus – Matthew 6:33

Ponderings

→ What is/are the object/objects of your faith?

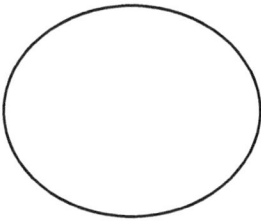

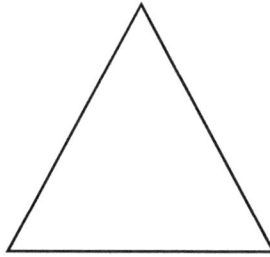

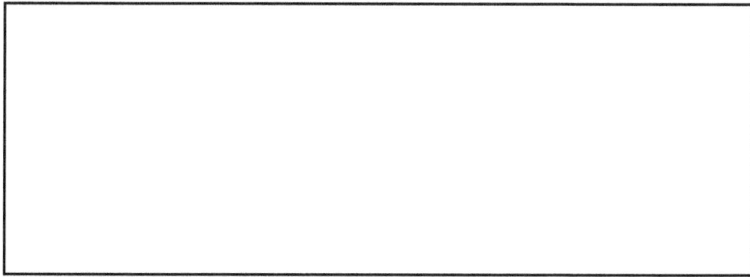

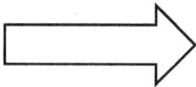

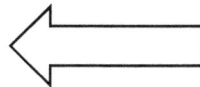

– 12 –

Secrets

*Don't only practice your art, but force your way into its
secrets; art deserves that, for it and knowledge
can raise man to the Divine.*

— Ludwig van Beethoven

According to the U.S. Census Bureau, 98.6 percent of American homes own a microwave oven.[27] Do you know the secret of the Microwave oven? The microwave was discovered by accident.

In 1945, Percy Spencer – an engineer at US firm Raytheon – was working with a radar machine when he noticed that a chocolate bar in his pocket was melting unnaturally fast. Realizing it must be connected with the microwave radio signals from the radar, he began experimenting with food and an electromagnetic generator inside a metal cage.

A few years later, Raytheon produced the first commercial microwave oven.[28]

What was secret about the microwave oven? Nothing really. Microwaves probably existed since the beginning of the electromagnetic spectrum.

Microwaves range in length from about one meter to just a few millimeters. They are part of the electromagnetic spectrum's wavelengths of light we can't see. From radio waves up through the very few waves our brain can interpret into visible colors – red, orange, yellow, green, blue, indigo, and violet[29] – to gamma rays, all these radiation wavelengths existed long before people "discovered" their frequencies.

The real secret was not that microwaves existed. The secret was how to uncover that which already was. What made microwaves a discovery is that for the first time Percy Spencer realized that that which existed, existed.

Secrets seem to dwell in two stages. One type of secret seats itself in a sureness of experience. A friend keeps the confidence of another. That's a secret.

A person hides an affair. Another hides their web browsing history. A family history that causes shame or embarrassment. A harmful habit. Debt. A criminal record.

The second kind of secret is something that exists waiting for an uncovering. Like gold embedded deep in the ground or sitting in plain view under the rippling waters of a flowing stream. The that just gold waits for someone to grasp it.

Once while standing in a deep gold mine shaft at Gold Reef City in Johannesburg, South Africa our guide asked, "Can you see it?" Looking at a wall in the hewn-out tunnel where we stood, not a single person in our group saw any gold in the rock face.

Then he pointed, "There it is." A small line of color difference ran through the rock surface in plain view. None of us recognized it. He explained that several tons of ore from that deep mine was needed to sift out just one ounce of gold. It was the reason the mine was turned into an amusement park as it was no longer a profitable mining venture.

In 1846, James Marshall along with his colleague noticed something shiny in a stream below a sawmill he constructed in California.[30] He wrote the account in his journal,

"What is it?" inquired Scott.
"Gold," I answered.
"Oh! no," replied Scott, "That can't be."
I said, "I know it to be nothing else."

In 1886, two prospectors discovered gold in Witwatersrand, South Africa. That gold unearthing marked a turning point for South Africa. At one-point, South Africa was the leading gold producer in the world.

Deep below the earth – 2.4 miles – the gold mine Western Deep No.3 Shaft in South Africa requires great expertise, effort, and danger to extract its valuable metal. South African mines are the deepest in the world.

True faith attempts to discover that which exists, yet seemingly remains buried in deep shafts of doubt, unfamiliarity, suffering, or pursuits of busyness. Faith approaches God who rewards focus upon him.

Yet, faith remains aloof buried in shafts of unfamiliarity for many sojourners of belief. They talk about faith, but see little practical evidence of it.

To see the unseen and experience its divine touch. That's worth prospecting for.

In Hebrews 11:6, lies 4 secrets to making God faith's object. Secrets that once enabled, energize faith's fullest capacities. As faith is energized, God responds with wonderful compensating rewards.

Four simply laid out principles explain faith. Four great – yet easy – secrets that will invigorate your faith. Four secrets enabling anyone to make God the object of faith thereby invigorating God's response to our faith. These principles are:

Faith Secret #1 – **Want God's Pleasure**
Faith Secret #2 – **Want God's Presence**
Faith Secret #3 – **Want God's Person**
Faith Secret #4 – **Enjoy God's Presents**

These four secrets will help you focus your faith upon God. In doing so, you'll experience meaningful interactions with God. Interactions that will help you grasp the realness of God; where God becomes tangible.

– 13 –

Faith Secret #1

Want God's Pleasure

And it is __impossible to please God without faith__.

— Hebrews 11:6

If we displease God, does it matter whom we please?

— Leonard Ravenhill
Why Revival Tarries: A Classic on Revival

The author of Hebrews made perhaps one of the more important statements of the Bible, "Without faith – *not a lot of faith* – it's impossible to please God." — Hebrews 11:6 Added Emphasis mine

Faith is quantified by its focus not its quantity. Paul just says "faith." Any amount of faith. Any depth of faith. Any description of faith. Just faith.

Why is this important? Now, please get this. It's important because faith is the only quality that pleases God. Gains God's approval. In this approval, God's rewarding compensation follows. A rewarding that requires only one simple gesture towards God; faith. Maybe a simple faith like:

A reaching up.
A look towards a different direction.
A first glance.
A first bike ride without training wheels.
A first kiss.
A first pet.
A first friend.
A walking away from the DMV with your first driver's license.
A first watching of a movie in a theater.
A first, "I love you."
A first baby.
A first pony ride.
A first college trip.
A first trip to another country.
A first exposure to another culture.
A first time to stand before an active volcano.
And, a first step in faith towards God.

Faith is like the seasoning in a pot of soup. Without spices the soup is bland and unpleasing. Few wish to partake of it. I think God might be like that.

Faith flavors our relationship with God. Without it our soup ekes out a bland concoction of unconnected stuff floating in our souls. Little appeal: a lesser reason to desire.

Pleasing God is the difference between an enriched meaningful connection with God, or just talking about God. Between a deep well of fresh cool water or a cup of disappointing expectation.

Faith is the key. Faith is the vital act unlocking God's pleasure as our faith directs us towards the Creator.

Let's wrestle with this statement for a moment. **"Without faith it's impossible to please God."** Without this intrinsic quality, God's lack of pleasure with me adversely affects my pleasure with him. If God is not pleased with me, how can I then find pleasure in him?

Maybe – just maybe – this is the reason that faith is such a kerfuffle for so many? Faith becomes a hard journey when it's actually an easy path to begin.

Faith's Easy Approach

It's not like God asks me to crawl on glass to pleasure Him. Or, hold a meditative position for hours on end. Or, like those devout Filipinos who crucify themselves on Easter to gain God's attention.[31]

Going over a barrel at Niagara Falls is impressive, but not to God... unless there's faith in that barrel as it drops over the cascading water's edge into the abyss below.

Those Weak-Faith Disciples. Jesus chided his disciples for their lack of faith, "Then he asked them, 'Why are you afraid? Do you still have no faith?'" — Mark 4:40

86

I think perhaps God is like this with me. With you. When faith is absent from our spiritual efforts, we throw our souls into the busyness of religiosity; something other than God.

Looking at the interactions recorded between Jesus and his disciples, it seems Jesus often tired of his followers lack of faith. To simply believe and follow.

I'm sort of taking the disciples side on this one. Think about it. To be one of the Twelve Disciples. Those who followed Jesus. Served at his every request. Expected to feed and put up with hordes of people trying to get close to him. Following Jesus was not easy I suspect.

And, what did their following get them? A stern rebuke, "Where is your faith?" Why? Because regardless of all the walking alongside of Jesus, without faith their efforts led to a dry meaningless connection to something other than Jesus. Without faith they just did Jesus' stuff rather than enjoy Jesus' soul.

I sort of hear Jesus talking to his disciples with the South African English accent I enjoyed hearing during my many years in Africa. "Ok chaps come heryah. Let's get it right. Faith first or you're totally finished."

Those Faithless Israelites too. In Numbers 13 and 14, Israel's lack of faith caused by their fear resulted in the eventual death of almost every adult. Seems a little harsh.

I mean, those Israelites left everything in Egypt, homes, jobs and security. Now in the desert they're asked to attack a militarily superior tribe. They're afraid. Who wouldn't be? Then wham! God says, "No faith, no Promised Land." Wow...

The entire 11th chapter of Hebrews lists scores of people who pleased God, and in return God compensated them in their adversities and struggles. Struggles not unlike our own today.

The Movie Series *Mission Impossible* comes to my mind. When faced with impossible odds, somehow Ethan Hunt and his team continually accomplish the impossible. Feats of incredible endurance and persistence leads viewers to believe that Ethan Hunt and his team can do anything.

Why? Because Ethan Hunt's team fully trusts Ethan Hunt. In return, Ethan Hunt rewards them throughout the movie. Remove any team member other than Ethan Hunt, and the movie survives. Take Ethan Hunt out of the screenplay, the movie flounders. Ethan Hunt is the focus.

Such is often the fate of faith. Remove the main player – God – and there is little to talk about. Our soul's scripts fall apart looking for meaning in other than God. Nothing else fills the God-whole in our souls.

Here's the deal. Take the greatest achievements of your life and look for the faith factors in them. Your dreams, aspirations, goals and accomplishments. Where is faith in the mix?

Without faith, all the God-stuff embarked upon doesn't count for much. Not to God. There's not much pleasure in it for God unless faith propels our actions.

Whether in the jungles of the Amazon feeding little orphan children or the CEO of the most successful company in the world – apart from faith – God's not impressed. Our God-stuff apart from faith is a soul falling short of God's intended best.

How could our paltry efforts alone please the One who created the universe? Look at the stars. Imagine the vastness of cosmos. Then look at yourself. Pretty discouraging. Huh?

Without faith it's impossible to please God. That little Greek word *adynatos* in Hebrews 11:6 implies "without strength, impotent, powerless, weakly, or unable to be done. Impossible."[32]

Now, let's turn this around. A galaxy is composed of hundreds of billions of stars. Our solar system is the stuff orbiting just one star; our sun. Our solar system is a tiny part of the Milky Way Galaxy.[33]

I'm a very small – extremely tiny – speck of dust upon a speck of dust in a solar system that is but a mere speck of dust among billions of other specks of dust in the universe.

What if, these minute specks – you and me – could gain God's pleasure simply by faith? And, what if that faith caught the attention of a Being expanding the universe?[34] My faith – your faith – causing God to express, "Hum, that pleases Me. You please Me."

Once, while sharing these thoughts, a friend responded, "Why would I be concerned about that?"

Why indeed? Why should I care whether God is pleased with me? The answer is, **"Because faith is reciprocal."**

Reciprocal Faith

Faith initiates a reciprocal pleasure response by God towards us. As we pleasure ourselves in God, God pleasures Himself in us. It is here that friendship develops. As Abraham became a friend of God because he believed in God, we too can we become God's friends. — James 2:23.

Friendship is reciprocal. What is friendship but two or more people certain of each other's mutual interests showing a willingness to invest time into each other? Few friendships exist between people who refuse to advance themselves towards each other. Friendships don't happen apart from a belief that time, energy and personage is worth investing into another.

Years ago during a furlough from our missionary work in Africa, we settled down to a year of life and service in Wisconsin. As I began to introduce myself to people in the church we decided to attend, a woman looked me directly in the eyes and said, "I'm not going to invest my time into a friendship with you and your family because in a year you'll be gone." Ouch.

Grandchildren are Reciprocal. To me, faith is like my grandchildren's magic words, "I love you papa." These words offer me such pleasure that this grandfather's love always reciprocates. A mere reaching up gains an immediate response. That response is often tangible.

One response landed me in a bit of hot water. As an early riser, I sat at the table of our oldest son's home very early in the morning before anyone awoke. Drinking my coffee, a small special presence approached from the side. There, my granddaughter said, "I love you papa."

After giving her a hug, I responded, "I love you too sweet pea." Then, I asked, "You want to have breakfast with papa? Just you and me? It will be our secret." She looked at me with her sleepy eyes lifting her head up and down.

I asked, "What do you want for breakfast?" A smile exploded from her face as she whispered, "Ice cream."

With that, a small bowl of chocolate ice cream was delivered before her beaming face.

Two hours later, my son upon coming down the stairs from his bedroom stopped abruptly, and with the voice of a disapproval piped, "Dad…"

There sitting at the table we – my grandchildren and me – enjoyed various flavors of ice cream for breakfast. Perhaps, that's the reason my grandkidos always ask, "Where's papa?" And, why there's never any ice cream in the house when we visit now?

All they need to do to capture my pleasure is to cast a smile towards me. Works every time. Faith is like my grandchildren's smile. An infantile belief that I am worthy to pursue. An innocent belief that garners my pleasure.

Faith like grandchildren. Faith is like crawling into the lap of the Creator reaching upwards with the innocence of a small child asking, "Who are you?"

Faith introduces us to God for that first time. Faith explores God's person. It is then, faith pleasures God.

Faith Misconceptions

Try making a list of all your positive contributions. That which you feel faith played a part. Here's mine written in my journals:

1. Good father – I try.
2. Good husband – I try here too.
3. Wonderful grandfather – pat me on the back!
4. Pay my bills.
5. Honest – except when I tell stories. Might exaggerate a wee little. Most pastors and missionaries do.
6. Compassionate – I try.
7. Generous – to a fault.
8. Sing meaningful worship songs…
9. Missionary work…
10. I pray…
11. Read the Bible…
12. My list goes on…

It's a fairly impressive list. At least to me. As I looked over it I thought, "Yah, God, I'm trusting you enough to do all these things." Then, I asked myself, "How much did faith actually play a part?"

A startling conclusion followed. If little faith accompanied any of these activities, they accounted for little. None of what I listed – zero, nada, zilch – pleased God apart from faith. That's a bit of a problem. Isn't it?

Whatever faith is, we better get it. If it that's the only ingredient to gain God's pleasure, then faith becomes a supreme consideration above anything else.

Hebrew 11:6 tells us that regardless of our efforts and accomplishments, anything outside of faith fails to impress God. All the difficult laborious efforts we try to do for God benefits little without faith.

Faith is like the icing on a cake in our interactions with God. Imagine if everything we attempted arose from a faith-effort. Take my same list a page back:

1. Good father by faith.
2. Good husband by faith.
3. Wonderful grandfather by faith.
4. Pay my bills by faith.
5. Honest through faith.
6. Compassionate through faith.
7. Generous through faith.
8. Sing meaningful worship songs in faith.
9. Missionary work… by faith.
10. Prayer in faith.
11. Read the Bible with faith.

Same activities with faith being the important distinction. In our daily life and activities, exercising faith – even the tiniest of amounts – gains God's pleasure.

Faith gains God's pleasure.
In pleasure, God responds to us.
It is then we can also pleasure ourselves in God.

Ponderings

1. Faith is reciprocal. Any thoughts?

– 14 –

Faith Secret #2
Want God's Presence

*Anyone who **wants to come to him**…*

— Hebrews 11:6

God can't give us peace and happiness apart from Himself because there is no such thing.

— C. S. Lewis

"Anyone who wants to come to him…" solicits a question. "What do you really want; Something from God, or God?" There is a monumental difference here.

The last time you approached God, what was your motivation for doing so?

I have a confession to make. Often, I come to God only after I've exhausted all other avenues of opportunity and effort. Then, the reason for my approach becomes more about wanting God to do that which I could not do for myself.

Much praying – I suspect – is more about wanting something from God than wanting God. Sort of reminds me of the kid that crawls up on Santa's lap during the Christmas season to read an exhaustive list of wants from Santa. Little interest exists in Santa, but only the possibility of Santa's gifts.

This is one of faith's attempts greatest flaws.

Wanting God only for what I perceive God can give me actually distances me from God. Wishing for God's presence only for His provision attempts to manipulate God.

Israel in the Old Testament modeled this detrimental pattern repeatedly. When in trouble they cried out to God. When they returned to God, God responded positively.

He blessed Israel. Then prospered Israel. God gave the nation health and strength when confronting their enemies, and just about every other good thing one can imagine.

Then, Israel fell in love with themselves again abandoning God for their hedonistic pleasures, power and prosperity. Israel found themselves separated yet again from God languishing in their own self-worth.

This type of faith – recorded in my journals – to me, looks like this:

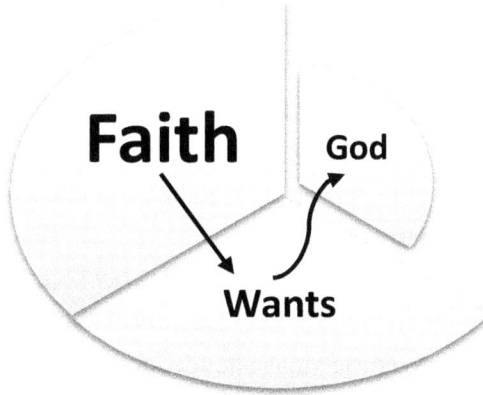

Sure, God encourages us to come to him with requests for help. In our time of need, the writer of Hebrew encourages us to approach God. — Hebrews 4:16

But, when approaching God, we need to look towards the Supplier more than the supplies. Towards the Provider more than the provided.

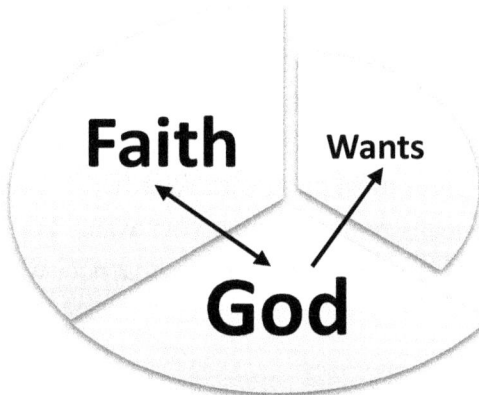

Once a Zulu pastor stood in front of his people at our church in St. Chad's Mission, South Africa. He led a prayer gathering. Those Zulu prayer gatherings in the mountains of Natal, South Africa didn't resemble any prayers I've ever heard in American meetings.

A Zulu woman asked for prayer. "Please pray," she said, "that this week enough food will appear to feed my children." The Zulu pastor's words caught my attention.

"God never leaves us or forsakes us. God is our source of food for both our stomachs and our souls. Let us approach God now."

So many of the prayer meetings attended in my many years with Africans witnessed a people with very little who made very much of God. In making much of God, God made much of them.

Wanting God is a foremost function of faith. God is always close. God is always present. God is everywhere. This is His intrinsic nature. Theologically, we used the term omnipresent to describe God's ever-present person.

God responds when we want closeness. James wrote about this:

Come close to God, and God will come close to you…

— James 4:8:

When want is centered upon God, Scripture tells us that God responds by drawing closer to us. Isn't that a great thought? When we center ourselves in God, God reacts in our favor.

Want and faith must align with God. The last time you sought God, was the focus primarily upon your wants from God or your want of God? The Apostle James argues that poor want is the reason prayers are weak, inept and unanswered:

*...when you ask, you don't get it because your motives
are all wrong—you want only what
will give you pleasure.*

— James 4:3

Faith's motive is everything. Faith wants God before other considerations. Faith thirsts for God presence.

My sons regularly contact me through various forms of media. In their late thirties, they still seek out their Father just to talk. "Hey Dad, how are you doing?" brings pleasure to this Dad.

A friend of mine shares a different story. His adult children regularly contact him as well. Their conversations begin quite differently than do mine with my sons.

He shared, "It really bothers me that the first words to come from my children's mouths is always, 'Dad, can you help me with this?'" By "help" they mean, "Dad, will you give me more money?"

My friend shared that his adult children's interest in him for mostly money, "Rips a hole through me."

These two diametrically opposed relationships reflect faith.

I've wondered if God feels the same way when we approach Him centered upon our wants?

I think God loves to hear, "Hey dad how's it going? How you are doing today?"

Wanting God means entering into His presence. Entering that presence takes practice.

Practicing the Presence of God

Nicholas Herman was a 17th century Carmelite Friar in Paris, France. On the battlefield during the Thirty-Year War – at the age of eighteen years of age – he underwent a deep conversion to Christian faith.

His friend and biographer described it in these words, "At that moment he saw clearly the Providence and Power of God,[35] … in the winter, seeing a tree stripped of its leaves, and considering that within a little time, the leaves would be renewed, and after that the flowers and fruit appear, he received a high view of the Providence and Power of God, which has never since been effaced from his soul."[36]

Nicholas became known as simply brother Lawrence. His lack of education disqualified him from the priesthood. Yet, he purposed to practice God's presence and love in every activity assigned to him at the monastery in Paris, France.

He was assigned to tasks he hated. Working in the kitchen as a cook, dishwasher and cleaner, he spent his life in the most menial of jobs. Yet, in the grunt labor of the monastery his sense of God's presence in his every thought, word, and activity became renown.

Surrounded by highly educated priests, bishops and vicars, people traveled from all over Europe to visit Brother Lawrence. He was the lowest of the low, yet, the most sought-after church celebrity of the day.

Monsignor Joseph de Beaufort, vicar general to the archbishop of Paris, became Lawrence's friend. As such, he complied writings of their many conversations together.

After Brother Lawrence's death in 1691, Beaufort published the book, *The Practice in the Presence of God*. The book was a favorite of John Wesley, the founder of Methodism.[37]

Brother Lawrence believed that even in the most unpleasant mundane of tasks, God's love surrounded him. Even in arduous activities, enjoyment could ensue if he realized God's presence and love surrounded him in all tasks.

Probably, the outstanding feature that encapsulated Brother Lawrence's life is bound in the words of the vicar, "He, always enjoyed himself no matter what he was doing because he did everything, even the smallest things, for the love of God. The trust he put in God honored Him deeply and drew great blessings."[38]

He continued, "The same was true of his work in the kitchen; to which he had a natural aversion. He proceeded to do everything there for the love of God, praying continually for God's grace to do his work well. In this manner, he had found everything easy during the fifteen years that he had been employed there."[39]

In another session, Brother Lawrence shared, "God's presence does not depend upon changing what we do, but in doing for God's sake what we normally do for our own sake."

Learning to practice the presence of God takes discipline, time and patience. Most of all, it requires want. Want of God more than anything else. A spiritual breath that desires God's presence in every activity.

My mornings often finds me in the early hours trying to meditate upon God's presence. "To persevere in the presence of God," as Brother Lawrence put it.

Now, I'm no Brother Lawrence, but I've learned that sensing God's presence requires refocusing thought and soul upon God – and God only. God's majesty. God's presence. God's grace. God's love. God's judgements. God's friendship.

Focusing upon the names of God in the Old Testament helps me think of God's presence. The names people in the Old Testament gave to describe God – Yahweh, the self-existent, eternal God – tell much of his person.

YHWH-Yireh — "Yahweh will provide" — Genesis 22:13-14

YHWH-Rapha — "Yahweh that heals" — Exodus 15:26

YHWH-Nissi — "Yahweh our Banner" — Exodus 17:8-15

YHWH-Shalom — "Yahweh our Peace" — Judges 6:24

YHWH-Ra-ah — "Yahweh is the Way, my Shepherd"
— Psalm 23:1

YHWH-Tsidkenu — "Yahweh our Righteousness"
— Jeremiah 23:6

YHWH-Shammah — "Yahweh is the Light, ever present"
— Ezekiel 48:35

God wants those who want him. When I practice the presence of God – I think – God practices the presence of Don. I'm not advocating some new guru principle. But… it does appear in Scripture that when people seek God's closeness, God responds in closeness towards them.

This thought is embedded in the Old Testament. When Israel sought God, they found God. God responded with kindness, care and protection. Look at these few examples:

The LORD is with you when you are with Him. If you seek Him, He will be found by you, but if you forsake Him, He will forsake you.

— 2 Chronicles 15:2

So tell the people that this is what the LORD of Hosts says: 'Return to Me,' declares the LORD of Host, 'and I will return to you,' says the LORD of Hosts.

— Zechariah 1:3

But as for me, it is good to draw near to God.

— Psalms 73:28

For many of us – I suspect – this depth of faith is unfamiliar. We are the faith-strugglers sitting in churches, small groups, and Bible studies seeking to make real what we try to believe suffocated in life's busyness.

Practicing the presence of God can change this frustration into a vibrant reality. Sensing God's presence brings realness to what we claim to believe because practicing God's presence embraces the Greatest Command:

Jesus replied, 'You must love the Lord your God with all your heart, all your soul, and all your mind.'

— Matthew 22:37

Ponderings

→ What does your faith really want?

→ What are your thoughts about practicing the presence of God?

→ How can you practice the presence of God in your life?

→ What does your faith chart look like:

– 15 –

Faith Secret #3
Want God's Person

...those who <u>sincerely</u> seek him.

— Hebrews 11:6

I like the Phillips translation of this verse,

And without faith it is impossible to please him. The man who approaches God must have faith in two things, first that God exists and secondly **that it is worth a man's while** to try to find God.[40]

This third principle begs a question, "**Is God worth our time to pursue**?" Not merely an attendance to religious or spiritual duty. A crowding of God into an already packed busy life. Is God worth our time to pursue before all other considerations?

There's a disconnect here. Isn't there? If we're honest with ourselves, many of us who identify ourselves as Christians spend time seeking God in conferences, seminars, fellowships, meetings and other activities. Do those activities bring us closer to God? The answer I'm often hearing is, "Not really."

Maybe, it's because we search for God like a bow on a wrapped gift. A garnishment to our efforts. Something to make us look pretty in all our religious busyness.

Think about it. When is the last time you spent any amount of thought or energy in pursuing God? In brutal honesty, many of us – most I suspect – pursue things about God, but rarely get around to the actual person of God.

When Labels Center Our Faith Conversations

Seems that when talking about God and faith, getting past labels present behemoth challenges. I'm not against names describing identities. But, somewhere in all the labeling and distinctives of our faith and churches, pursuit of God gets lost.

As a missionary traveling and visiting churches around the world first responses tell me a lot.

I'm Baptist, Catholic, Presbyterian, Lutheran, Methodist, or Brethren name just a few. Charismatic, Jesus-only, reformed, orthodox, fundamentalist, traditional, biblical, bible believing, or fill

in the blank_____.

Somehow in the good church stuff, God gets lost in our souls with all the tags used to describe what we believe. We never seem to get around to talking about why we believe what we believe.

Upon my first month in South Africa years ago, a Zulu pastor expressed a dumbfounding answer to a question. I asked, "What is the greatest need of your congregation?" He responded, "To translate and teach the Westminster Confession of Faith to my people."

Looking at his people with shoeless children and inadequate housing, his answer left me astonished.

Another friend once shared with me that every Christian ought to know and recite often the Nicene Creed.

I thought, "Hum, where does that leave me who – as a young Catholic boy – learned The Apostles' Creed?"

Let's talk about Christ's beautiful Church a bit. Christ makes the Church beautiful. Yet, in all the labels we affix to the Church, sensing God's presence becomes our soul's casualty.

Trigger Warning. Some next considerations may offend more sensitive viewers. Viewer discretion is advised.

Charismatics. Many charismatics – a wonderful group of people – consider it very worthwhile to pursue the Gifts of the Spirit. They believe all the gifts are in effect today.

Like a horse out of the gate at a derby, often the first question asked me is, "Have you ever spoken in tongues?" Frequently, when talking with charismatic people we rarely navigate far from speaking in tongues.

It appears that in exhibiting these gifts, the gifts often – not God – become the object of faith. It's an easy pit to fall into.

Meeting a friend for coffee, he mentioned a mutual acquaintance. He said, "Our friend drilled into me about his visions, tongues and the such the other night. Lasted a good two hours. Man! If he'd talk as much about Jesus as he talks about tongues, now that'd be something."

Many lovely Charismatic people pursue gifts to such a degree that the gifts is all one hears. Where is God in all of this?

Evangelicals. Evangelicals describe themselves in broad terms as Biblical literalists. They believe in salvation by faith alone in Christ's atonement – covering over – for our sins.

The very word "evangelical" has its roots in the Greek language of the New Testament meaning "gospel" or "good news." They believe in decisional faith. Meaning, a person must decide to put faith in Christ before actually becoming a Christian.

Evangelicals possess a high regard for biblical authority. They fight over different views of prophecy, biblical inerrancy, infallibility, Calvinism verses Arminianism, and Election verses Free Will.[41]

As a missionary – seeking to raise support – I've visited over 300 evangelical churches. It's interesting to listen to the messaging of a church.

You'll hear about the mission of the church. The church's distinctives, life groups, membership classes, dynamic worship, or the different ways you can financially give to the church.

"Come as you are!" marks the mantra of the trendier churches. Yet, upon leaving church you'd hear little of the Church's owner: Jesus Christ.

Now, I'm not an old fart who stands against every new genera of worship style or outreach. My question is simply, "Where is God in it?"

Reformed. Reformed Theology is a rising movement in circles today. The word "alone" partially identifies its theology:

- By Scripture alone
- By faith alone
- By grace alone
- Through Christ alone
- To the glory of God alone[42]

These are wonderful truths. The challenge is that when speaking to someone who is reformed, the conversation can rarely get past "reformed" to Jesus.

Reformed becomes the fulcrum upon which every spiritual conversation swings. It's difficult to talk about the worthwhileness of pursuing God when a first consideration is, "Are you reformed?"

Once embroiled in such theological systems – it seems to me – we relegate God to our own little theological boxes. Faith gets lost in the mix.

Then there's the Catholic side of me. Raised in the Catholic faith, I often caution fundamentalists and evangelicals of making rash statements about Catholics.

Once as I sat in a McDonald's in Big Bend, Wisconsin, a man sitting in another booth pretty much forced his presence upon me. He volunteered that he belonged to a large Bible believing mega-church in the area. Then out of the blue he started talking about Catholics.

The intrusion was most irritating. In his anti-Catholic utterings he proclaimed, "My biggest problem with Catholics is that they worship Mary."

I shot back, "NO, that is not correct. Catholics venerate Mary. They don't worship Mary." He replied, "What's the difference?" Gruffly I replied, "EXACTLY."

My demeanor caught him off guard when as I asked him to leave me alone.

There's are a lot of things I love about the Catholic Church. Liturgies, reverence in worship, solemnness of the mass, the majesty and architecture of the old glass stained cathedrals, and respect for leadership.

However, many conversations with Catholic relatives and friends rarely seems to navigate past "Catholic" to "Christ." The two terms seem synonymous. I'm Catholic therefore I'm a God-follower. Catholic equals Christian.

Then, there are the political voices in the Church. One says, "I don't see how you can be a Christian and vote for a Democrat." Another cries, "Republicans do not love or care for people. True Christians vote for Democrats."

I can say this with utmost confidence, "God is neither Democrat nor Republican." In fact, God is not American: white, brown or black.

Isn't this the dilemma of much of Christianity today? Getting past what we believe about God to focus upon the God in whom we believe?

In all the talking about God, we never really seem to get close to God. We focus on names, distinctives, and differences more than actual pursuit of God.

When I was a young man an old evangelist spoke about Knowing God. In his message he started with, "Let me talk to you about God. I've known him for a very long time." Wow.

Preaching and teaching today seemingly centers around what I call the 4 M's: Methods, Masses, Money and Me.

Historical Christianity centers upon, "I believe in God, the Father almighty, Creator of heaven in earth. . ."

Most Christianity today scores a 10 out of 10 here in God-belief. We excel in, "Anyone who wants to come to him must believe that God exists…" — Hebrews 11:6c

Yet, when it comes to God-knowing, the bottom drops out of our faith a bit.

Getting to know a person. The first few times I met my spouse – Kathy – created an impression. Enough that I asked to spend time with her.

Up to that point, Kathy was just Kathy. I'd seen her, and acknowledged in my mind that she existed. If one asked about the petite young woman named Kathy, I believed in Kathy. Kathy-belief indicated that a person named Kathy existed. She stood 4ft. 11inches tall. Her eyes were blue.

Kathy-pursuit led towards Kathy-knowing. The more time we spent together, the greater my desire for her. This knowing didn't come from statements about Kathy. Or, a conference on *How To Know Kathy*.

Forty years later, she is the one person above all others I desire to know. Kathy-belief led to Kathy-pursuit. In pursuit, I know Kathy.

My relationship with God contains similar bearings.

God's presence acknowledges that God is everywhere. In prayer, God is there. In Bible reading, God is there. When I reach out in desperation, God is there. When I ask, God is there. Seeking God's person goes from simply acknowledging God towards an approaching of God.

How does one get to know this God? This is found at the end of Hebrews 11:6:

> *...who sincerely seek him.*
> I like the King James Version,
> *...them that diligently seek him.*

The phrase "diligently seek" in Hebrews 11:6 is from the Greek word *ekzeteo* carrying power-packed meanings. It implies zealously seeking for something with all of one's being. It presents the picture of one who seeks something so passionately and determinedly that one literally exhausts all power in the search.[43]

That kind of faith resembles the History Channel's show *The Curse of Oak Island*. Here, two brothers from Michigan – Rick and Marty Lagina – purchased part of this island.

Legend tells of the Knights Templar leaving England – perhaps 800 years ago – with 13 ships loaded with gold and burying those riches on Oak Island in Nova Scotia, Canada.

Another theory claims the missing French Crown Jewels of Marie Antoinette are buried on the island too.

For more than 200 years, treasure hunters flocked to this small island in Mahone Bay, hoping to find an alleged treasure buried on Oak Island.[44]

Rich and Marty continue to look for a treasure that six people lost their lives for over the past 200 years. Even President Franklin D. Roosevelt financed a dig.[45]

Oh, that I might want God more than any gold buried on Oak Island! Wanting God's person so much that I center myself upon the company and person of God before all other considerations.

Centering yourself in God. Have you ever quieted yourself in a noiseless environment and just contemplated God? Taking the truths of Scripture about God, trying to center yourself in God?

How great you are, Sovereign Lord! There is no one like you, and there is no God but you, as we have heard with our own ears.

— 2 Samuel 7:22 NIV

For every house is built by someone, but God is the builder of everything.

— Hebrews 3:4 NIV

Taste and see that the Lord is good;
blessed is the one who takes refuge in him.

— Psalm 34:8 NIV

Since you are my rock and my fortress,
for the sake of your name lead and guide me.

— Psalm 31:3 NIV

We love because He first loved us.

— 1 John 4:19 NIV

Let's take the last verse, "We love because He first loved us." A centering thought while pondering God is, "God how do you love?"

This places God as the subject of faith. Contemplating God's love helps draw me towards His Person.

Another Scripture is a great example, "I can do all things through Christ him who gives me strength." — Philippians 4:13 NKJV

Centering thoughts, "How can I do this or that through Christ? What do I need to do? What kind of strength?"

Prospecting for God

God's response is contingent upon the degree and quality of our seeking him. **"Sincerely seeking God"** is what faith pivots upon. When studying this phrase an old man came to mind.

During my early years as a young intern pastor, an old gentleman visited the church in Dallas where I attended. His appearance interested me. Short and slight of build – in his cowboy boots and hat – he sported one of the best handlebar mustache's I'd ever seen.

Asking him of his employment, he told me, "I'm a prospector." The answer caught me off guard. "A what?" I answered. He smiled, "You know a prospector. I look for gold." Over the months he attended the church, he told much of his life as a gold prospector.

Once I asked him, "What's the intrigue? Why?" His smile lifted both sides of his mustache as he responded, "There's just something about the search. Pan after pan of nothing from creeks and small rivers. In every pan, the anticipation of maybe this time."

He showed me a very small gold nugget he carried with him. As he lifted the small glass tube from his pocket, there at the bottom of the tube a small kernel of gold glistened in the water filling the tube.

The word seek here in Hebrews 11:6 carries of an idea of seeking, searching, investigating, scrutinizing, craving, or begging.[46]

Prospecting for God – if you please – is the primary function of faith. "Sincerely" implies that the seeker exerts considerable effort and care in learning something.[47] Like that old man prospecting for gold, faith's prospecting is an anticipation of discovering a renewed richness in God.

Going to my soul-streams often prospecting for God is where I want to be. Searching for God finds me panning often for the presence of God, focusing my wants, desires and aspirations upon Him. To want God more than life itself. More than those around me. More than the approval of others. Above income, activity and life's busyness.

Prospecting for God's person reveals God to me and in me. Sensing God's presence rather than just acknowledging it draws out golden nuggets of God's person. This is the challenge of faith. To want God above all else.

Ponderings

→ Where do you spend your efforts looking – panning – for God? Two essential ingredients are necessary:

Time –

Place –

When's your time? Where's your place?

→ When was the last time you experienced the presence of God?

→ How might you prospect for God's person?

– 16 –

Faith Secret #4
Enjoy God's Presents

*...he **rewards***
– recompenses, compensates and bestows upon –
those who sincerely seek him.

— Hebrews 11:6 Added Emphasis Mine

Six simple words appeared in my journal, ***"God Rewards Don Who Seeks Him."*** A faith-shift occurred in my belief.

Rather than simply circling around important belief systems instilled in me, my soul sailed towards God. As I sought pleasure in God, God reciprocated.

God became my rewarder. The New American Standard Bible translates the verse, "He is a **rewarder** of those who seek Him." The word "rewarder" spurred an adventurer's spirit to discover more!

The thrust of the word carries the idea of God paying wages. The old word used is "recompense." To recompense one for their activities, labors or efforts.

Seeking God requires dutiful activity. When faith pleases God, he compensates the faith bearer. Gives a reward. A recompense. A compensation for faith.

Again, in my journal I wrote, *"God rewards me when I seek him."* This personalized and applied faith's truth.

Wow! I can please God through faith.

When I please God, God responds.

When God responds faith is real because God is real.

I like to call this compensation for my faith, **God's Presents**. Focusing faith upon God showers me with his presents. This invigorates my faith.

In the past, as a veteran missionary living in Africa for more than two decades, faith was my game. I claimed to know faith. To live faith. I talked a big faith-walk.

I taught faith. Led people to faith. Carried myself in faith. Yet, deep inside I sensed a lack of faith in many considerations of life. That Day mentioned in the first pages of this book began to change faith's intensiveness.

Instead of focusing upon myriads of details involved in entering missionary service again, I purposed to focus primarily upon God. God above all, in all, and through all.

Details needed implementation to achieve our goal of entering the new designation of Missionary to Missionaries. One of the biggest challenges was raising our support – finances – to support of lives and ministry.

We – Kathy and I – purposed that God came first. Jesus' words bubbled to life again.

Seek the Kingdom of God above all else,
and live righteously,
and he will give you everything you need.

— Matthew 6:33

As we struck out on deputation again – the arduous task of raising money to support our missionary work – I finished my book, *To Hell, Back, and Beyond – A PTSD Journey: When Faith and Trauma Collide.*

Finishing of the book marked a huge faith-step. The book sought to answer, "How does faith exist in people suffering from severe trauma, and how can faith enable a person to turn a deficit into a strength?" *The Faith Principle* garnered new hope even in PTSD:

God compensates those who sincerely
and genuinely seek him, even in pain.

Compensates for life's injuries.
Compensates for life's traumas.
Compensates for life's betrayals.
Compensates for personal failures.
Compensates for private sins.
Compensates for income inequality.
Compensates for risking it all to start all over again.
Compensates for taking small steps forward.
Compensates for all issues of life.

Most of all, compensation for seeking God above all else. Making God my highest worthwhile priority. Faith became more about God and less about me. More about his Person and less about this person.

God in my situation. God in my affliction. God in my desires. God in my wants. God, the object of my needs. God in my mediations. God in my concerns for family. Faith brought God to my soul's front line. Rather than surrounded by the cares and troubles of life enveloping the soul, faith focused upon the One above all those things.

Centering myself upon God as the only object of faith brought God's response: His presents. This is the message of Hebrews 11:

It was by faith that Abel brought a more acceptable offering to God than Cain did. Abel's offering gave evidence that he was a righteous man, and God showed his approval of his gifts. Although Abel is long dead, he still speaks to us by his example of faith.

It was by faith that Enoch was taken up to heaven without dying— "he disappeared, because God took him."

It was by faith that Noah built a large boat to save his family from the flood. He obeyed God, who warned him about things that had never happened before.

By his faith Noah condemned the rest of the world, and he received the righteousness that comes by faith.

It was by faith that Abraham obeyed when God called him to leave home and go to another land that God would give him as his inheritance. He went without knowing where he was going. And even when he reached the land God promised him, he lived **there by faith**—for he was like a foreigner, living in tents.

And so did Isaac and Jacob, who inherited the same promise. Abraham was confidently looking forward to a city with eternal foundations, a city designed and built by God.

It was by faith that even Sarah was able to have a child, though she was barren and was too old. **She believed** that God would keep his promise.
And so a whole nation came from this one man who was as good as dead—a nation with so many people that, like the stars in the sky and the sand on the seashore, there is no way to count them.

It was by faith that Abraham offered Isaac as a sacrifice when God was testing him. Abraham, who had received God's promises, was ready to sacrifice his only son, Isaac, 18 even though God had told him, "Isaac is the son through whom your descendants will be counted."
Abraham reasoned that if Isaac died, God was able to bring him back to life again. And in a sense, Abraham did receive his son back from the dead.

It was by faith that Isaac promised blessings for the future to his sons, Jacob and Esau.

It was by faith that Jacob, when he was old and dying, blessed each of Joseph's sons and bowed in worship as he leaned on his staff.
It was by faith that Joseph, when he was about to die, said confidently that the people of Israel would leave Egypt. He even commanded them to take his bones with them when they left.

It was by faith that Moses' parents hid him for three months when he was born. They saw that God had given them an unusual child, and they were not afraid to disobey the king's command.

It was by faith that Moses, when he grew up, refused to be called the son of Pharaoh's daughter. He chose to share the oppression of God's people instead of enjoying the fleeting pleasures of sin. He thought it was better to suffer for the sake of Christ than to own the treasures of Egypt, for he was looking ahead to his great reward.

It was by faith that Moses left the land of Egypt, not fearing the king's anger. He kept right ongoing because he kept his eyes on the one who is invisible.

It was by faith that Moses commanded the people of Israel to keep the Passover and to sprinkle blood on the doorposts so that the angel of death would not kill their firstborn sons.

It was by faith that the people of Israel went right through the Red Sea as though they were on dry ground. But when the Egyptians tried to follow, they were all drowned.

It was by faith that the people of Israel marched around Jericho for seven days, and the walls came crashing down.

It was by faith that Rahab the prostitute was not destroyed with the people in her city who refused to obey God. For she had given a friendly welcome to the spies.

Faith brings presents – gifts – from God. As we focus our adoration towards God, God trusts us with his gifts. Faith keeps God's presents in the proper priority in our lives.

In little faith, few presents come from God. One of the most troubling verses for me is found in Matthew 13:58, "And so he did only a few miracles there because of their unbelief." God didn't give those people the best because of their lack of faith. No faith no presents from God.

Once Kathy and I brought Christmas gifts to a group of small orphan Zulu children in Steadville, South Africa. The gifts weren't much. Totaled a couple hundred dollars at best. Just pencils, pens, erasers, and a toy for each child.

The joy witnessed that day at the reception of those humble gifts still brings a smile to my soul. The hugs and smiles received guaranteed our presence and presents the next year. Faith is like that.

Faith pleasures God. It doesn't take a lot. But, it does require a sincere attempt. God's presents is exactly what makes life and faith an incredible journey to tell.

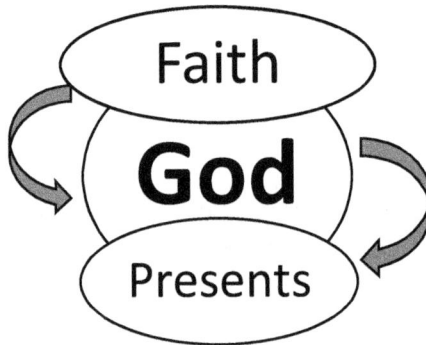

Faith

God

Presents

Ponderings

Can you think of 3 God-compensations in your life? Presents – rewards – for your faith?

Faith

God

Presents

What's in a Reward?

Faith is to believe what you do not see; the reward of this faith is to see what you believe.

— Saint Augustine

When God compensates faith, there is always purpose: God's purpose.

God is always the goal. If nothing comes from God other than his presence, that is reward enough.

Approaching God believing in the creator's enormity, and that in doing so, God rewards with direction and purpose marked out our new journey.

That Day in Honduras with those missionaries marked a week filled with faith and purpose to seek God above all else.

I wrote in my journal:

"God, we're starting all over again late in our lives. Our next steps feel like they're heading towards nowhere. But, you've called us to this new venture. Clearly, your leading asks us to look away from the glitter of what we want, towards You who promises to reward us as we actively seek you."

Faith put the house in the woods up in Northern Minnesota in the rearview mirror of desire as we focused forward. Soon we traveled to Fort Worth, Texas.

We walked into a former church that partnered with us during our many years in South Africa. It was during their Wednesday night Bible study. Mike – the senior pastor – saw us enter. He erupted, "Don, hey, so good to see you! What are you guys up to these days?"

After a brief explanation, he exclaimed, "Great. Share that in our Adult Bible Fellowship tonight."

After a brief verbal presentation of Missionary to Missionaries, Mike asked for a church business meeting on the spot. They voted to support us at $100.00 per month.

Kathy looked at me with a smile and her blue beaming eyes. My soul whispered, "Ok, God… you've got this."

After three years of raising funds, living in Missionary Housing across a dozen states, traveling to seven countries encouraging literally hundreds of missionaries, a message came to us.

The message read, "You need to call this lady. She is interested in what you're doing."

After a call, we sat with a couple we'd never met discussing an unbelievable possibility. Residing on Lake Granbury, Texas the couple regularly offered several of their chalets to people in ministry who needed a time of respite, rest and soul care.

They shared, "We want to do something special for missionaries." I asked, "What are you thinking?"

Walking us through to the edge of their property, we stood looking at a derelict old cabin. "We're thinking, what if we renovated this and called it 'Shepherd's House?'"

My initial thought was, "What a wreck of a place."

Yet, seeing the makeovers to their other chalets gave me confidence that the renovations might prove spectacular.

Then they added, "Of course, we'd need a missionary couple on site to bring in the right missionaries needing the most care. To serve them, care for them, and offer them respite."

My soul leaped, "You've got to be kidding God! You can't be this good."

As a boy raised in Minnesota – The Land of 10,000 Lakes – water holds a special place for me. I've always dreamed of being able to live on a lake someday. **The Faith Principle** spoke:

Don, God compensates your sincere faith in Him. Compensation to experience God's purpose, plans, and provision for your life.

Recently, my oldest son – Donnie – called while sitting on the porch of our cabin on a beautiful Texas lake – a property we did not purchase nor pay to rent – I described the surrounding scene.

Boats passed by on the lake outside the small harbor in front on our cabin. The long glorious covered porch in front of the house shaded us from the sun. Chinese geese swam in front of me. Egyptian geese flew in the distance. A Gray Heron to the left perched motionless on the bank searching the waters for its next meal.

Then Donnie added, "It's everything you talked about when we were kids dad. The lake, the cabin, and the boat." Oh, forgot to mention the pontoon boat sitting on the boat lift to the left of the cabin. A gift given to provide respite, rest and restoration to missionaries.

Missionaries helping missionaries work through the really tough stuff of missionary life and ministry.

Faith does that…

My mind never goes back to the yellow house in the woods of Northern Minnesota I loved so much. There is no place I'd rather be then where I am right now. God is the perfect paymaster, compensator and rewarder giving exactly what is due based on faith expended towards him.[48]

So, here we are – Kathy and me – living in a lovely cottage on Lake Granbury. We care for missionaries who come to us for rest, a listening ear, guidance, and healing. It's reward enough just to serve God and others, yet God adds his presents to remind of his goodness.

Twenty missionaries – plus their children – stayed with us the first year. That was in-between missionary retreats to Honduras, El Salvador and Haiti. This year we travel to Kenya, Tanzania and South Africa.

We are well content in life. Secured in God's grace. Fulfilled in God's purpose. Motivated towards another day. It's a great place to be in our final chapters of life.

It started for me with my discovery of *The Faith Principle* and its 4 secrets:

- **Want God's Pleasure** above all else.
- **Want God's Presence** more than life itself.
- **Want God's Person** more than yourself and others.
- Then, **enjoy God's presents.**

My friend, approach God often believing that He does actually exist and care for you. His care centers not upon you, but rather in his purpose and plan for you.

Want God above all else, and God will reward you with His pleasure, purpose and love.

Because above all else – please remember – God is most pleased when we center ourselves in Him.

*But without faith it is impossible to **[walk with God and]** please Him, for whoever comes **[near]** to God must **[necessarily]** believe that God exists and that He rewards those who **[earnestly and diligently]** seek Him.*

— Hebrews 11:6 Amplified Bible
Emphasis Mine

Other books by Don Mingo

Boundaries – 5 Steps to Getting Your Life Back. Helping people overcome pornography addiction with God's help. Faithway Publishers, Available at Amazon in paperback and Kindle.

For special rates contact at <u>donmingobooks@gmail.com</u>

Life Boundaries – Balancing Career, Marriage, Relationships, and the Important Stuff of Life. Available at Amazon in paperback and Kindle.

Get Your Life Back! Journal. A 21-week addiction renewal journal. Available at Amazon in paperback and Kindle. Also available at Barnes and Noble.

Son Risings – Discovering and Caring for the Real You. A book about soul-care. Available at Amazon in paperback and Kindle.

So, You Want to Be A Missionary: Essential Considerations. Available at Amazon in paperback and Kindle.

To Hell, Back and Beyond: A PTSD Journey – When Faith and Trauma Collide. Available at Amazon in paperback and Kindle. Also available at Barnes and Noble.

[1] Robert L. Thomas. *New American Standard Exhaustive Concordance of the Bible: Including Hebrew-Aramaic and Greek Dictionaries*, A.J. Holman, 1981. The University of Michigan, June 9, 2010. ISBN 0879811978, 9780879811976.

[2] Gerhard Kittel; G W Bromiley; Gerhard Friedrich: Theological Dictionary of the New Testament. Grand Rapids, Mich., Eerdmans ©1964-©1976. Vol. 4. Pages 695-798.

[3] Ibid.

[4] Katie Orr. *Everyday Faith: Drawing Near to His Presence*. New Hope Publishers. 2016 ISBN 1596694610. 9781596694613.

[5] https://mentalhealthgracealliance.org/christian-mental-health-and-mental-illness/battling-anxiety-spiritually

[6] https://nationalinterest.org/blog/buzz/russias-doomsday-submarines-are-here-armed-nuclear-robot-torpedoes-53947

[7] https://www.spaceanswers.com/q-and-a/will-we-ever-travel-faster-than-light/

[8] https://www.forbes.com/sites/startswithabang/2018/04/25/hubbles-greatest-discoveries-werent-planned-they-were-surprises/#36bae4035713

[9] https://www.space.com/39815-hubble-suggests-universe-expanding-faster-study.html

[10] https://www.express.co.uk/news/science/1162808/big-bang-theory-how-old-is-universe-physics-news-astronomy-space-2019

[11] https://en.wikipedia.org/wiki/Occam%27s_razor

[12] https://www.space.com/24781-big-bang-theory-alternatives-infographic.html

[13] https://www.huffingtonpost.com/entry/religious-celebrities-in-hollywood_us_55eb1d3ce4b093be51bbb192

[14] https://www.deseretnews.com/top/3671/0/20-athletes-who-are-vocal-about-their-faith.html

[15] https://dictionary.cambridge.org/us/dictionary/english/indirect-object

[16] https://www.merriam-webster.com/dictionary/indirect%20object

[17] http://www.softschools.com/examples/grammar/indirect_object_examples/77/

[18] http://www.dailygrammar.com/Lesson-191-Indirect-Objects.htm

[19]https://www.monergism.com/blog/prosperity-gospel-global-epidemic

[20]

http://www.onepassionministries.org/transcripts/2017/12/5/concerning-faith-romans-117

[21] https://en.oxforddictionaries.com/definition/reality

[22] https://en.oxforddictionaries.com/definition/hope

[23] https://en.oxforddictionaries.com/definition/evidence

[24] https://en.oxforddictionaries.com/definition/unseen

[25]

https://www.google.com/search?safe=active&q=Dictionary#dobs=hypostasis

[26] https://dilbert.com/strip/1999-03-01

[27]

https://www.census.gov/history/www/homepage_archive/2015/october_2015.html

[28]

https://www.newscientist.com/article/2141981-eight-great-accidents-in-scientific-discovery/

[29]

https://study.com/academy/lesson/visible-spectrum-definition-wavelengths-colors.html

[30] *"James W. Marshall's account of the first discovery of the Gold".* www.malakoff.com. Retrieved 20 May 2019 on Wikipedia https://en.wikipedia.org/wiki/James_W._Marshall

[31] https://www.cnn.com/2016/03/25/asia/philippines-easter-good-friday-crucifixion/index.html

[32]Thayer, Joseph H., Thayer's Greek-English Lexicon of the New Testament (Hendrickson Publishers Peabody, MA, reprinted 2000) https://www.studylight.org/desk/interlinear.cgi?ref=57011006

[33] http://astroweb.case.edu/ssm/100f08/astr100f2008hw1.pdf

[34] https://www.space.com/39815-hubble-suggests-universe-expanding-faster-study.html

[35] Brother Lawrence. The Practice of the Presence of God in Modern English. Translated by Marshall Davis 2013. ISBN-10:0989835065 (ebook)

[36] Herman, Nicholas, The Practice of the Presence of God, The Christian Classics Ethereal Library as quoted from https://en.wikipedia.org/wiki/The_Practice_of_the_Presence_of_God#cite_note-fulltext-1

[37] Brother Lawrence. The Practice of the Presence of God in Modern English.

[38] Ibid.

[39] Ibid.

[40] https://www.biblegateway.com/versions/JB-Phillips-New-Testament/

[41] https://en.wikipedia.org/wiki/Evangelicalism

[42]   https://www.christianity.com/church/church-history/the-five-solas-of-the-protestant-reformation.html

[43] https://renner.org/diligence-is-required-for-success-in-god/

[44] https://www.cbc.ca/news/canada/nova-scotia/curse-of-oak-island-reignites-centuries-old-treasure-hunt-1.2532813

[45] Ibid.

[46] https://www.studylight.org/desk/interlinear.cgi?ref=57011006

[47] https://www.preceptaustin.org/hebrews_116-7

[48] https://www.skipmoen.com/2007/04/new-testament-rewards/